THE MODERN GENTLEMAN'S HANDBOOK

# The Modern Gentleman's Handbook

EBURY
PRESS

Published in 2021 by Ebury Press, an imprint of Ebury Publishing,
20 Vauxhall Bridge Road,
London SW1V 2SA

Ebury Press is part of the Penguin Random House group of companies
whose addresses can be found at global.penguinrandomhouse.com

Text © Charles Tyrwhitt Shirts Ltd 2021
Cover design © Studio Polka 2021
Text design © Jonathan Baker 2021
Illustrations © Matthew Hollings 2021

Writer: Jo Bryant
Editor: Camilla Ackley
Production: Sian Pratley

This edition first published by Ebury Press in 2021

www.penguin.co.uk

A CIP catalogue record for this book is available from the British Library

ISBN 9781529108842

Printed and bound in Great Britain by Clays Ltd, Elcograf S.p.A

Penguin Random House is committed to a
sustainable future for our business, our readers
and our planet. This book is made from Forest
Stewardship Council® certified paper.

'YOU HAVE BRAINS IN YOUR HEAD.
YOU HAVE FEET IN YOUR SHOES.

YOU CAN STEER YOURSELF IN ANY
DIRECTION YOU CHOOSE.

YOU'RE ON YOUR OWN, AND YOU
KNOW WHAT YOU CAN DO.

AND YOU ARE THE GUY WHO'LL
DECIDE WHAT TO DO.'

**DR SEUSS**

# Contents

# Foreword

I had been thinking about writing a book for many years. Everybody should write one, shouldn't they? It was going to be about my life in shirts. I am still not sure how I ended up in the wonderful world of men's dressing – it was never meant to be like that. It was supposed to be a life on stage – preferably in front of a million adoring fans in Rio de Janeiro.

Like many, life has not worked out quite how it was supposed to. Having done geography at university (and no geographer has a clue what to do when they 'grow up'), all I knew was that I didn't want to be a town planner.

I did know that I have always loved shirts. We had a New & Lingwood down the High Street at school and I used to love popping in just to feel the beautifully soft two-fold Egyptian poplin shirts (and their brightly coloured socks, but that's another story). There is something magical about a crisp cotton shirt – I feel total solidarity with Daisy weeping over Gatsby's beautiful shirt collection. That could so easily have been me.

In 1986, I started Charles Tyrwhitt. Perhaps I should have done computers or mobile phones, but I didn't love either of those things. I loved shirts. I loved clothes. I loved dressing. We evolved into suits and ties and cufflinks and then trousers and waistcoats and shoes. The pandemic moved us on into casual clothing and even hoodies! The world is now changing so fast that it is becoming increasingly confusing to know what to wear when, but I do hope this book will act as a trusted guide.

It has been a glorious life of colourful characters and ups and downs. Like all rag traders, I have been through booms and busts. I have been taken to the cleaners but have somehow always managed to bounce back. Like all entrepreneurs, I am the eternal optimist. Good times are always just around the corner. I am never satisfied – things can always be better. Nothing is ever perfect.

More than anything, that applies to how we behave and how we dress. I marvel at the mysteries of dress. What to wear? When to wear it? How to wear it? The emotion, the complexity, the fun that can be had from dressing. It is quite amazing how dressing the part, looking the part and behaving the part can make the difference between a life of unending excitement and opportunity and a life of abject disappointment.

After 35 years, I have seen a lot and I was beginning to wonder whether my book should perhaps be more about the art of dressing and behaving – a modern gentleman's handbook – rather than tales of the toil and struggle of survival in the rag trade.

So, when I was approached by Ebury Publishing, it seemed like the right time to put together less of the story behind the brand, but more a book to help others to 'get it right' and to consign those ridiculously embarrassing situations that can befall any one of us to history.

I defy anybody to read this book and not learn a huge amount! I wanted it to be fun. Dressing is fun and it is as much about the individual as anything else. Behaviour is a different thing altogether. Get it wrong and you will burn bridges that can never be rebuilt. I do hope this book will make you laugh in places, but I also hope it will help you to build bridges and to become an infinitely better version of yourself.

And if you are already perfect, then I hope that you might find people in your lives that will benefit.

**NICK WHEELER, FOUNDER - JUNE 2021**

# Professional

❖———❖———❖

## THE SHIRT • THE SUIT • TAILORING
## TIES • POCKET SQUARES
## THE BLAZER • THE SMART TROUSER
## SHOES • COATS

'STYLE IS WHEN THEY'RE RUNNING YOU
OUT OF TOWN AND YOU MAKE IT LOOK
LIKE YOU'RE LEADING THE PARADE.'

**WILLIAM BATTIE**

# Ahead of the Game

When it comes to first impressions, it's more about how you look and less about what you say. No one takes the bad dresser seriously – dressing the part can up your game personally and professionally, so the right shoes might just be the thing to help get your foot in the door, and on and up the professional ladder.

The rules may have relaxed in recent times, but getting it right still requires some care and attention to detail. If that all sounds like too much hard work, then think of it like this: wear clothes that fit you properly and always look better than the next guy.

Whether you're a rookie learning the ropes or a big shot with a corner office, if you manage a touch of style and flair then you can confidently head into Monday looking the part – and that's half the battle won, however your week is shaping up.

# The Shirt

## AN ODE TO THE SHIRT

A good shirt is *never* wrong. Ever. If the office is formal, a good
shirt is essential – and the better ones give you an indefinable
difference. If the office is casual, a good
shirt stands out against the T-shirts.
And if the office is somewhere
in between, a good shirt is
always better than an OK
or bad one.

Formal, casual, at work,
at play, at dinner, at breakfast,
out and about or at home, a good
shirt always works. The same
good shirt can be crisp and smart,

laid-back and relaxed, focused or unfussy. It just depends on how you work it.

You can wear a good shirt with a suit, you can wear it with a blazer, or soften it with a cashmere jumper or merino zip-neck. You can wear it with jeans or chinos, you can wear it with suit trousers, you can stick it on with shorts. You can wear a good shirt with a tie, or keep it open-necked, or roll up the sleeves.

In short, everything starts with the shirt.

---

**KEEP YOUR SHIRT ON**

In the mid-1800s, your average man only had a couple of shirts. If he found himself in a skirmish, he would remove his shirt and battle it out bare-backed to preserve his scant wardrobe. If he kept his cool and bypassed the brawl he had, as we still say today, managed to 'keep his shirt on'.

---

## SHIRT ESSENTIALS: FITS, CUFFS AND COLLARS

### Three Fits

~ *Classic:* Traditional and roomy – big in the back, chest and shoulders. Back pleats offer more comfort. Good for more rotund builds, particularly if on the shorter side.

~ *Slim fit:* The go-to for most men. Wider through the chest and tapering to the waist – creating a pleasing V-shape –

while allowing comfort and plenty of room for those who aren't in the gym 23 hours a day. If in doubt, start here.

~   *Extra slim fit:* Sharp and streamlined, this is the ideal shape for those in shape themselves. Slim across the chest, arms and waist; it is contemporary and fitted. Avoid if carrying a little timber.

**FYI** *The front of your shirt should be flat, crease-free and close-fitting (without being too tight). The back is where the room is – the more space you need at the front, conversely, the bigger the back to the shirt. The yoke (bit across the top of the shoulders) should touch the edge of the shoulders.*

## Four Cuffs

~   *Double cuff:* Formal, traditional, and fastened with cufflinks. For important meetings, weddings or black tie. The patriarch of cuffs.

~   *Rounded cuff:* Modern and functional, but smart and business-like. A gently curved cuff to be fastened with one or two buttons. For work shirts and casual shirts – a solid all-rounder.

~   *Mitred cuff:* Like the rounded cuff, but more angular and cut away. Still professional, but more contemporary and less classic, and can be one- or two-button. A younger look.

~   *Adjustable cuffs:* As above, but with a button on the gauntlet (the gappy bit on your wrist above the cuff-fastening). Button it up for a tighter, smart fit. Unbutton for a looser fit. Generally for more casual shirts.

(FYI) *On formal shirts, cuffs should pop out of the end of a suit jacket, but not flap around your fingers – roughly 10–12cm from the tip of your thumb is where to aim.*

## Four Collars

~ *Classic:* The traditional collar for the traditional shirt. Never wrong. Suits a classic four-in-hand tie-knot and a traditional tie. Your first port of call if in doubt.

~ *Cutaway:* With collar points sharply angled outwards, it's a more modern look for those who prefer a fatter tie-knot – but also works well with no tie at all.

~ *Semi-cutaway:* Between the classic and the cutaway, it's the ideal collar for a shirt doubling up for formal or casual wear. Works with a tie, works without a tie – it can be dressed up or down.

~ *Button-down collar:* A staple of Oxford shirts, it's a softer, more casual look – great tieless with a blazer or V-neck jumper.

(FYI) *You should be able to slide your fingers between neck and collar. For structure, always use collar stiffeners (unless it is a button-down collar).*

## THE MULTITASKER: ONE SHIRT, FIVE WAYS

*One crisp white and one sky blue shirt can be all you need ...*

~ *Meeting:* Button it up, stick a tie on it, chuck a jacket on.

~ *Lunch:* Leave the top one or two buttons undone, chuck a blazer over the top.

~ *Desk:* Leave the top one or two buttons undone, pair with a merino zip-neck or cashmere V-neck.

~ *Pub:* Keep tucked in or untuck (careful that it is not too long), unbutton the neck (not too far there, Elvis), roll the sleeves to high forearm.

~ *Weekend:* Unbutton the neck, roll the sleeves to mid-forearm, chuck on a pair of jeans and throw a friendly sweater over the top. Relax.

**FYI** *An extra bottom button can help keep shirts tucked in properly; on a formal shirt, the tails should be long enough that they don't ride up and hang out.*

---

'THERE IS NO IRON IN THE IRON
YOU USE TO IRON SHIRTS.
WHICH IS, IRONICALLY,
BOTH IRONIC AND UN-IRONIC.'

**JEREMY IRONS**

## LIFE SKILL: HOW TO IRON A SHIRT

Dry-cleaning might sound like the successful man's shirt care of choice, but it will damage the fibres and decrease their lifespan. Wash at 40°C (unless the label specifies otherwise), inside out and with non-biological detergent. Before you iron, make sure the shirt is unbuttoned (including the cuffs) and slightly damp – it's best to use a steam iron.

~ *Collar:* Pull taut; start with the underside. Iron from each outside edge to the centre, then fold along the neckband seam and iron to create a fold.

~ *Cuffs:* Start on the inside, working from the outside edge to the centre, and then repeat on the outside. Fold double cuffs in half, cufflink holes aligned, and iron to form a crease.

~ *Yoke (shoulders and upper back):* Start from one shoulder – put it over the thinner end of the ironing board – and work towards the centre. Turn the shirt around and repeat.

~ *Sleeves:* Spread out a sleeve, with the cuff-opening facing upwards. Iron from the underarm seam down towards the cuff. Turn over and repeat, then repeat on the other sleeve.

~ *Back:* Smooth over the width of the ironing board and work from the yoke down.

~ *Front:* Fit the top of the armhole over the thinner end of the ironing board and iron the front; repeat on the other side. Work your way downwards in sections, ironing between each button.

~ *Finally:* Button up to the top and hang immediately to dry or you'll undo all your hard work.

---

### WHY MEN ARE RIGHT

Women's shirts button on the left, whereas men's button on the right. Why? Because women used to be dressed by their maids, and it's easiest for a right-handed person to button up another person from the left. Men had the tough job of dressing themselves, which is easiest done from the right (unless you're a leftie, which makes the simplest of things topsy-turvy).

'THE ONLY THING STANDING BETWEEN YOU AND YOUR GOAL IS THE BULLSH*T STORY YOU KEEP TELLING YOURSELF AS TO WHY YOU CAN'T ACHIEVE IT.'

**THE WOLF OF WALL STREET**

## YOUR NAME IN LIGHTS: PERSONAL BRAND

It is a common misconception that 'personal brand' is about promoting yourself, when really it is much cleverer than that. It is a powerful mix of perception and reputation, with a goal of being seen as a leader in your field, no matter how big or small that may be.

You can control most of it, such as how you communicate, interact, respond and react to different situations, and you can work on what people see when they type your name into Google. And then there is the one thing you can always curate – your image and how you dress.

Fundamental to it all are your values and the things that really matter to you. Your experiences, professional journey, achievements and failures all culminate to create a unique and powerful story, but it is important to remember that a personal brand is always evolving – we are all works in progress.

# The Suit

## THE THREE STYLES

### The Italian

Lightweight, sleek and the most fitted. Trousers are very slim; the jacket is tapered at the waist. Shoulders are unpadded, pockets are flapless and piped.

~   *Who's it for?* Smaller-framed men.

### The American

Looser and boxier, also known as the sack suit. The jacket is straight with roomy sleeves and a single back vent; the trousers are fuller.

~   *Who's it for?* Bigger men.

### The British

Structured and elegant. The jacket is tapered at the waist, with slightly padded shoulders, side vents at the back and slanted, flapped pockets. Trousers are slim (but not skinny) and sit high.

~   *Who's it for?* All body shapes.

'THE SUIT IS A WINDOW TO THE SOUL:
LIGHTWEIGHT COTTON WHEN CASH
IS TIGHT, ITALIAN CASHMERE WHEN
AN INHERITANCE LANDS; WAISTLINES
DRAWN IN DURING ILLNESS OR ANXIETY,
AND LET OUT AT TIMES OF EXCESS.
WEDDINGS, FUNERALS, CHRISTENINGS,
AND COURT APPEARANCES – ALL OF LIFE'S
LANDMARKS ARE SANCTIFIED, QUIETLY
AND CONFIDENTIALLY, BY ONE'S TAILOR.'

**BEN SCHOTT, *JEEVES AND THE KING OF CLUBS***

## THE FOUR CUTS

**Single-button.** Though not the most traditional, it is clean, elegant and streamlined. Great for a shorter man (it lends the impression of height) or for a skinnier man (it draws the eye to the middle fastening), but one to avoid for a rounder man.

**Two-button.** If in doubt, go two-button. The most traditional and flattering, it sits well on medium, bigger or smaller bodies.

(FYI) *The bottom button is just for detail and should never be done up.*

**Three-button.** An older, more formal cut that is less common now. They close higher up the chest, helping taller men create more of a statement, but do widen the top of the torso – making them less than ideal for broader men.

(FYI) *On a three-buttoned suit, do up the middle one only (though doing up the top one too isn't technically wrong).*

**Double-breasted.** A great suit for a slim man as they add width and build. Avoid if you are short (they will look boxy) or large (they can make you look bigger).

(FYI) *Some leave the bottom button unbuttoned – Prince Charles doesn't, though, and he knows about double-breasted jackets.*

## ON SCREEN: ICONIC SUITS THROUGH THE DECADES

**1940s: Humphrey Bogart, *The Maltese Falcon* (1941)**
Classic charcoal-grey pinstripe, double-breasted with peaked lapels. The sartorial credit is all Bogart's – actors back then usually provided their own costumes.

**1950s: Cary Grant, *North by Northwest* (1959)**
A grey three-button classic, noticeably worn for most of the film. Some say the film's more about what happens to the suit, rather than Grant's character.

**1960s: Steve McQueen, *The Thomas Crown Affair* (1968)**
A lesson in how to wear a three-piece. Undeniably British and of the era: a two-button with notch lapel in Prince of Wales check, effortlessly paired with a five-button waistcoat. Iconic.

**1970s: Robert Redford, *The Great Gatsby* (1974)**
A dark chocolate-brown pinstripe three-piece. Not something everyone can get away with, but the vintage yellow Rolls-Royce helped, not that Redford needed any.

**1980s: Al Pacino, *Scarface* (1983)**
'Say hello to my little friend' … the bold gangster-inspired pinstripe three-piece, perfect for a 1980s drug lord meeting his fate.

**1990s: Robert De Niro, *Casino* (1995)**

Take your pick. Pink, green, grey, blue, beige …

45 bespoke suits were made for De Niro and the costume budget was rumoured to be one million dollars.

**2000s: Daniel Craig, *Casino Royale* (2006)**

A dark navy wool three-piece, with a light pinstripe.

A fitting suit – albeit slightly looser-fitting than Craig's later 007 suits – for a scenic finale on Lake Como.

**2010s: Colin Firth, *Kingsman: The Secret Service* (2014)**

A selection of double-breasted perfection, albeit with bullet-proofing. The film tells us, 'The suit is the modern gentleman's armour' – literally in this case.

## SUIT STYLE: BUSINESS VS OCCASION

The business suit needs to do a few things: it must create an air of professionalism, be smart and hard-wearing. It is worn often in a variety of places: the office, on commutes, around town, etc. It takes a fair beating so should be made well, of sturdier fabric, and of muted tones to be more versatile.

It should never be fun. That's where the occasion suit comes in – every man should have at least one suit that is only for time off, functions and parties (but never call it your party suit). It should have a touch more flair, a little more *élan*. It could be a one-button, a touch tighter, perhaps more Italian than British.

But, really, what's important is how it makes you feel. It should not be like pulling on the office uniform; instead, there should be that whisper of excitement, a night out, two (or three) too many drinks, and a foggy morning after. Just as the business suit is a statement of who you are in the office, the occasion suit is who you are out of it.

## FOUR OF A KIND: SUIT DETAILS

~ *Weaves:* Plain or birdseye is the standard, traditional suit cloth. When you have more confidence, try experimenting with herringbone, cross-hatching or twill.

~ *Checks:* A bold choice for a business suit but can work for an occasion suit, if you have the personality to pull them off. Prince of Wales check looks particularly good on a double-breasted suit.

~ *Stripes:* Generally, the bigger you are, the thicker the stripe you can take, but keep it under control. Too thick and you get a bit 1920s Chicago gangster (and you'll have a job finding the spats to go with it). A vertical stripe, subtly interwoven, helps add the impression of height and can elevate a suit from sober to sophisticated.

~ *Cloth:* Watch the weight: 8-ounce cloth is for a lightweight, summer suit (and hot climes); 12-ounce is a good all-year, all-rounder; 14-ounce is for a heavyweight, winter suit.

## POCKET THE DIFFERENCE

Suit pockets on a British suit are slanted largely for traditional reasons – it allowed for easy access when on horseback; it's also why they have flaps, as they helped keep out dust and dirt. The ticket pocket (a second, smaller pocket above the main pocket) was a hallmark of the country suit, offering gentlemen somewhere for their train ticket as they escaped London. Nowadays you don't need one, but it is a stylish detail and somewhere to put your travelcard.

## LIFE SKILL: HOW TO CARE FOR YOUR SUIT

**FYI** *Correct cleaning and storage of your suit will keep you looking sharp, and extend its lifetime.*

~ *Maximise your investment:* Trousers show signs of wear more quickly than jackets, so consider buying two pairs.

~ *Be supportive:* Hang your jacket on a wide, thick hanger that is the correct size for the shoulders. Fold your trousers in half with the seat pockets on the outside, and drape over the bar of the hanger (avoid using hangers with clips).

~ *Three-day week:* It's not just you who needs some downtime. A suit should be given 24 hours of breathing time between each wear.

~ *Hang loose:* Give it plenty of room in the wardrobe and use breathable garment bags to protect it.

~ *Brush it off:* Brush hanging up, unbuttoned, with a soft, natural-fibre clothes brush after every wear. A lint roller can be useful for stubborn specks.

~ *Get steamy:* For everyday creases, hang your suit in the bathroom when you shower – the steam acts as a de-wrinkler. Never use a household iron; if you want to keep things extra smooth, invest in a home steamer.

~ *On the spot:* Suits should not be dry-cleaned more than twice a year as it weakens fibres and risks fabric going shiny.

**FYI** *Spot-clean small stains with baby wipes.*

~ *Clean up:* Seasonal suits should be dry-cleaned before they are stored for any long period of time. Food and sweat particles can attract moths, so it's best to put them away clean.

## ETIQUETTE SOS: JACKETS ON/OFF

~ British jacket etiquette is much more 'keep it on' than 'take it off'. If in doubt, leave it on.

~ In a meeting, don't be the first to take off your jacket (unless you're the boss, then you set the agenda). It's not an alpha move, it just looks cocky.

~ If it's really hot, take your cue from the most senior people in the room. If they seem fine, you may just have to cope.

🛈 *Always undo suit jacket button(s) when you sit, and always do them up when you stand.*

## SIX STEPS TO OFFICE SUCCESS

**'Never burn bridges. Today's junior pr\*ck, tomorrow's senior partner.' –** *Working Girl*
*Be the nice guy:* From the bottom of the food chain, right to the top, keep everyone onside. Say 'good morning', ask about weekends, remember kids' names, chat to the front desk and acknowledge junior employees. You never know when you might need a favour – or be flung together – so play nice.

**'What we've got here is failure to communicate.'**
**–** *Cool Hand Luke*
*The name game:* Remember that crushing feeling when someone forgot your name, or couldn't recall that you'd met before? Don't compromise your own success with such a simple error. Pay attention during introductions and help a name to stick by repeating it during conversation. There's nothing worse than being lost for words during a later introduction.

**'There's nothing cheap about loyalty.' –** *Up in the Air*
*Play it straight:* Gossip is dangerous, breaking confidences professional suicide. Be genuine and be your (professional) self. Reliability, dependability and competence are likely to get you that promotion – boot-licking reverence will not.

**'You just have to accept that some days you are the pigeon, and some days you are the statue.' – *The Office***
*Know who's boss:* There is always a pecking order. Don't cross the line with those who are more senior than you; they are always your boss and, when the chips are down, rarely your (true) friend.

(FYI) *If you are introducing two people, always introduce the more senior to the junior (for example 'Laura [chief executive], this is James [intern]'). It will make them feel suitably important, even if they don't realise it.*

**'Sorry I'm late, I was saving the world. You know how it is.' – *Ant-Man***
*About time:* Meetings in the UK always start on time. Being late is needlessly self-important and plain rude. No one cares how busy you are – being late just tells them that you think that their time isn't as important as yours.

**'It's not personal. It's strictly business.' – *The Godfather***
*Essential email:* Use proper grammar and spelling; watch your tone; be cautious of humour; strike a balance between friendly and formal. Before you hit send, do the essential checks: read what is lurking at the depths of the email trail and, most importantly, assess who *really* needs to be copied in – keep it on a strict need-to-know basis or you'll lose your audience.

# Tailoring

*When buying a shirt or suit, there are three ways to go – fully bespoke, off-the-peg or made-to-measure.*

**Fully bespoke:** Start with an empty page and go from there: it is a design entirely concocted between you and your tailor. If you want nine pockets on one side and none on the other, then you can make that happen. Three arms? Go for it. They are expensive and luxurious, but a total one-off, custom-made for your size, shape, measurements and whims. Nobody else in the world has a suit or shirt exactly like this.

**Off-the-peg:** Self-explanatory – it is a shirt or suit designed to fit the average man, so S, M, L and XL. Sleeve lengths can be tweaked, waists altered and trousers taken up but, basically, what you see is what you get.

**Made-to-measure:** Somewhere between the two, sometimes known as semi-bespoke. The tailor will have a pattern that they will customise to your measurements, meaning you get a shirt or suit that fits you like a glove. You can choose fabric, colour, weight, weaves, collars, cuffs, monogramming, buttons and even thread colour. The result? An immaculately well-fitted shirt or suit for a fraction of the price of fully bespoke.

'THE ONLY PERSON WHO ACTS SENSIBLY IS MY TAILOR. HE TAKES MY MEASURE ANEW EVERY TIME HE SEES ME. EVERYONE ELSE GOES BY THEIR OLD MEASUREMENTS.'

**GEORGE BERNARD SHAW**

## SUITS YOU: BUYING A MADE-TO-MEASURE SUIT OR SHIRT

~ *Don't be intimidated.* You're paying the money and you'll be the one wearing it. If you feel like a tailor is guiding you somewhere you don't want to go, or blinding you with terminology, say something or you'll be the one living with the consequences.

~ *Give them detail.* Tell the tailor what your job is, whether you sit in the office or travel around, or whether it's for the summer or winter. The more they know, the better they can tailor it to you.

~ *Get their advice.* Tailors are experts in knowing what suits you: it is literally their job to make you look good, and they might suggest something you hadn't thought about.

~ *Be real.* When you are being measured, there is no sense in sucking your tummy in or puffing out your chest. You'll get something that doesn't fit you, and that somewhat defeats the point.

~ *Enjoy it.* How often in life do you get something tailor-made just for you and at such a reasonable price? A made-to-measure shirt will come in around the £100–200 mark. There is not much else at such a price that is custom-built for you and you alone.

## ICONS: TAILOR TO THE STARS – DOUG HAYWOOD (1934–2008)

A legendary Savile Row tailor from humble working-class Cockney beginnings, Doug Haywood's unaffected, natural charm, along with his extraordinary tailor's eye, led him to dress the great and the good. His 1960s Mount Street premises became a destination in its own right as a tailor's, an ad hoc private gentleman's club and an impromptu party house. His client list included Terence Stamp, Terry O'Neill, Roger Moore, Sir John Gielgud, Steve McQueen, Clint Eastwood, Richard Burton, Mick Jagger, Peter Sellers, Bobby Moore and Rex Harrison, to name a few. His lifelong friend and client Michael Caine said Haywood's manner and attitude influenced his role in Alfie; John le Carré said Haywood shaped the character of Harry Pendel in The Tailor of Panama. His master cutting can be seen in the suits he styled for *The Thomas Crown Affair*, *The Spy Who Loved Me* and *The Italian Job*.

## IN THE KNOW: BRACES

~ Braces create a streamlined silhouette, allowing the trouser to hang naturally from the waist (especially flattering for expanding waistlines). They improve posture, gently reminding you to stand tall and straight.

~ Classic colour choices are black, navy or brown; patterns and colours can add a touch of flair when glimpsed under a suit jacket. Clip-ons are more convenient; purists opt for buttoned.

~ 'Belt and braces' might be the well-known phrase, but never wear both with a suit.

~ Braces are called 'suspenders' in America. Don't get confused with something that should sit firmly in a date-night underwear drawer.

## WAISTCOAT WISDOM

Worn right, a waistcoat can work some magic by adding structure to your suit, slimming larger builds, bulking up smaller builds (especially when double-breasted) and balancing out short legs and long bodies. Make sure it is neither too tight nor too loose – comfortably snug, but no straining buttons.

There are a couple of waistcoat rules to live by: avoid wearing a double-breasted waistcoat under a double-breasted suit – it will be hot, bulky and look old-fashioned – and never pair a waistcoat with a belt (too bulky) or a tie-clip (too fussy).

And then there are the two commandments that must never be broken … First, no shirt should ever show between your waistcoat and waistband and second, always leave the bottom button undone. If you remember nothing else, remember this.

'YOU'D BETTER ANSWER THAT.
IT COULD BE SOMEONE IMPORTANT.'

**QUEEN ELIZABETH II (WHEN SOMEONE'S
MOBILE PHONE RANG DURING A MEETING)**

## MAKE MEETINGS COUNT

The meeting to meet, to test the water, to seal a deal, to float an idea, to drop a bombshell, to fire, to hire, to congratulate … the meeting about a meeting. Every meeting may be different, but they all have the same hope: to serve a purpose and be over quickly.

To help things along, you need to play your part. Be on time and at least look like you've glanced at the agenda. Don't digress too much and, if things aren't ticking along, steer everyone back towards the purpose of the meeting.

If things start to drag, watch yourself. Meeting fatigue can quickly set in, but even a hint of bored body language may offend present company. Equally, watch the signals from the other players around the table: if you are losing them, you need to speed up and prioritise. Once they start to check their phones, you've lost them completely. You, of course, would never touch your technology - it is basic good manners to prioritise your company over your devices, no matter how pressing your screen alerts are.

# Ties

## TO WEAR OR NOT TO WEAR?

It used to be pretty simple – if you are wearing a shirt, then wear a tie. Today's dressed-down offices and more relaxed functions make life complicated, but remember that even with looser dress codes, a tie will never be wrong. You can wear a tie with jeans, chinos and, of course, a suit – as long as you've got a shirt on, a tie will still look right.

The suit-with-no-tie look softens the impact of a suit, and works for evenings, for outdoor events, for parties, and for some offices and meetings. It looks great with a pocket square, too. But only you can know what works in your world – so take your lead from others, rather than taking the lead and underdressing at the wrong moment.

Functions are more complicated but you can always remove a tie and stick it in your pocket if others are all open-necked; it's much harder to conjure one up if you find yourself suddenly in need.

## TIE RULES

~ The four-in-hand knot is the go-to knot; the slightly chunkier half-Windsor is useful for a thinner tie or a wider collar. Ignore the full-Windsor – it's the fattest of knots that never passes muster.

~ Your tie-knot should occupy your collar comfortably, without overfilling it.

~ A broad-shouldered man can take a wider tie, while a slimmer man suits a skinnier tie (and smaller collar) but avoid extremes – too wide and it looks like a bib, too narrow and you may as well not bother.

~ Length matters: when tied, your tie should just hit the waistband of your trousers. Don't tuck it in, don't leave it hanging Donald Trump-style halfway down your flies.

~ Bright colours add flair, adventure and pizzazz, but keep them on a tight leash. Your tie should be at least a shade darker than the shirt, and never, ever lighter.

~ Play with textures: woollen, knitted or grenadine ties offer a more interesting, tactile and softer look. Wool and cashmere ties work well in winter; silk and linen are best in summer.

~ Match ties to occasions: a business meeting is no time to be playful; a wedding is no time to be business-like.

~ Never go novelty. *Ever.*

'BOND MISTRUSTED ANYONE WHO TIED
HIS TIE WITH A WINDSOR KNOT.
IT SHOWED TOO MUCH VANITY. IT WAS
OFTEN THE MARK OF A CAD.'

**IAN FLEMING, *FROM RUSSIA WITH LOVE***

## LIFE SKILL: TIE CARE

Remove your tie by untying it in the reverse order to which you tied it – a touch tedious, but those few extra minutes will add years to its lifespan. For quick storage, loosely roll it up, with the small tip innermost and the wider end on the outside. Better still hang it up.

Never iron a tie; remove wrinkles by hanging it in a steamy bathroom. Be cautious of over dry-cleaning and spot-remove stubborn stains. Blot or dab with water, try an organic baby wipe or, for greasy marks, apply talcum powder, leave for a while before brushing off and gently wiping away any remnants with a damp cloth.

# Pocket Squares

## EYE FOR DETAIL: HOW TO FOLD A POCKET SQUARE

*Practice makes perfect: a well-folded pocket square should never bulge your breast pocket. A pocket square should never match your tie.*

### Beginner: The square pocket square

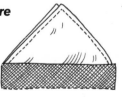

Fold your handkerchief in half twice so it forms a square, then in half again to make a triangle. Next, fold in the two long opposite points of the triangle and then tuck the pointed end into your jacket pocket so only the straight edge shows.

~   The look: classic, clean, understated

### Intermediate: The one-point pocket square

As above, fold your handkerchief in half twice to form a square, then half again so it forms a triangle. Again, fold in the two long opposite points of the triangle. Instead of leaving the straight edge showing, turn it around so the top of the triangle shows.

~   The look: the square pocket square with a dash of flair

### Advanced: The two-point pocket square

Fold your handkerchief in half twice so
that it forms a four and one-half inch
square. Lay it on a flat surface with one
corner pointing up and one pointing down, like a diamond.
Fold the bottom corner up so it sits on the left of the top
corner, to form two peaks sitting side by side. Fold each side in
towards the middle, and tuck the straight end into your pocket.

~   The look: Formal, elegant, old-school charm

### Quick: The puff pocket square

Fold your handkerchief in half twice and
lay it on a flat surface. Pinch the middle
of the square and lift up. Tuck the excess
fabric into your jacket pocket, leaving the pointed
edge showing.

~   The look: Curated casual

### Takes practice: The reverse puff pocket square

This is an upside-down puff pocket
square. You simply create the puff
pocket square as above, but instead of tucking the excess
fabric into your jacket pocket, leave it hanging out.

~   The look: Quietly flamboyant

'TO ACHIEVE NONCHALANCE,
WHICH IS ABSOLUTELY NECESSARY
FOR A MAN, ONE ARTICLE AT
LEAST MUST NOT MATCH.'

**HARDY AMIES**

## TAKE FIVE: THE BUSINESS LUNCH

The ambience will make or break a good lunch. Straining to hear each other in a buzzing brasserie is a recipe for disaster, but equally white-tablecloth formalities can make clients clam up. Strike a balance.

You may be a ramen junkie, spice addict or tapas fan, but choose a straightforward, crowd-pleasing cuisine or you risk making your client feel uncomfortable or, worse, foolish if they are unfamiliar with it all.

Don't leave them hanging. Arrive before they do; make sure they can spot you easily, or that the front desk knows you are expecting them. Seat your guests with the best view, not facing the wall.

Pipe up promptly if there are different menus on offer – for example, 'The set lunch looks great today, shall we go for that?' – before they blow your budget on the lobster thermidor.

Settle up the bill quietly away from the table rather than flashing the plastic in front of your guests.

# The Blazer

The problem with the blazer is that the word has a fustiness – the school blazer, the club blazer, the brass-buttoned blazer – which belies the fact that it is the single most versatile and useful item in a man's wardrobe.

You can chuck a blazer over almost anything and it will elevate your look. You can wear them everywhere, too: the office, the pub, a Sunday walk, a restaurant, the school run. The same jacket works in high-powered meetings and a night on the town with your mates.

Pair with jeans and T-shirt for acceptable going-out attire. Upgrade the T-shirt to a shirt, and the blazer makes you date-ready. Chuck it on over a shirt and chinos or jeans to elevate your work outfit to a more sophisticated smart casual. Add a tie, and you can take that important meeting. All while wearing the same jacket.

> 'I'M A JACKET MAN. I DON'T KNOW
> HOW TO OPERATE IN SHIRT SLEEVES.'
>
> **BILL NIGHY**

## BLAZER RULES

~ The versatile, must-have everyday blazer is blue or grey, single-breasted and woollen.

~ Two buttons is classic, one button is elegant, three buttons is too many and double-breasted is for your dad.

~ Classic fit is a roomier, more comfortable option; slim fit is sleeker but may not work for every build.

~ Once you have the staple all-rounder in your wardrobe, play about with fabrics and patterns – cashmere, textured wool, subtle herringbone, linen … the options are (almost) endless.

> 'THE PRIME NECESSITIES FOR SUCCESS
> IN LIFE ARE MONEY, ATHLETICISM, TAILOR-
> MADE CLOTHES AND A CHARMING SMILE.'
>
> **GEORGE ORWELL**

# The Smart Trouser

## CHINOS

Not as smart as a suit trouser, not as dress-down as jeans – chinos are the perfect in-betweener that comfortably bridge the gap between work smart and work casual. Pair with a jacket and shirt for semi-formal office days; match with a merino knit and shirt for relaxed work-from-home days; stick with an Oxford shirt for a more casual – but still professional – look.

For a flattering, modern silhouette, opt for a slim fit – but bigger men can benefit from a looser, more traditional style (but don't let them get too baggy). Aim for flat-fronted, non-iron chinos for true style and practicality. There is a colour for everyone too, from darker and neutral or, for the sartorially bold, brighter shades for a brave colour pop. The classics, though, don't go out of style – sand, khaki and navy are rarely wrong.

# Shoes

1.  Brush or wipe off any loose dirt. Remove laces and insert shoe trees.

2.  Apply a nourishing shoe cream in circular motions with a soft cloth. Remove any excess and leave for 20 minutes or so.

3.  Apply a proper wax polish with a brush (avoid quick-fix liquids). Start with the edges then work your way around the shoe in firm, circular motions, finishing with the upper (top). Use a toothbrush for fiddly areas.

4.  Leave for a few hours, preferably overnight, to allow the polish to work its magic.

5.  Wipe off any excess with a cloth before vigorously buffing with a softer brush.

6.  Admire the shine.

---

**ALL IN A NAME: BROGUE**

Invented to drain the water from shoes worn on Scottish and Irish bogland, brogue is the name for the distinctive perforated pattern seen across many styles of formal shoes. Originally solely for outdoor or country-wear, they became inner-city staples in the 1980s but now work as both formal wear with suits and more casually with jeans (particularly in tan, often as a boot too).

---

'BEFORE YOU JUDGE A MAN, WALK A MILE IN HIS SHOES. AFTER THAT, WHO CARES? HE'S A MILE AWAY AND YOU'VE GOT HIS SHOES.'

BILLY CONNOLLY

## BEST FOOT FORWARD: FORMAL SHOES

### Look Smart: The Oxford

The classic, go-to formal shoe, with distinctive closed lacing (i.e. no eyelets on show). Lace horizontally and only wear with a suit or formal trousers. The smartest Oxfords are black and plain-toed (and patent plained-toed worn for black tie, see p.51); toe-cap Oxfords have a line of horizontal stitching or brogue perforations. Oxford brogues can be boardroom black, a casual brown or a smart casual brown suede.

### Essential Versatility: The Derby

Seamlessly switching between formal office shoe and smart casual work/weekend staple, the Derby is a true multitasker. Smooth leather in black or brown are the most formal, and chunkier styles, with thicker soles, pair well with chinos and jeans. There are plenty of Derbys with eye-catching detail, from two-tone colours to broguing and contrast stitching, but consider if you want your clothes or your shoes to be the highlight of your outfit. It needs to be one or the other, not both.

### Stylishly Different: The Monk Shoe

Characterised by smooth lines and bold buckle detail, the monk shoe partners well with a slim-legged trouser and flourish of coloured sock. They will always stand out more than an Oxford or Derby – the truly confident could try a double buckle.

### Laid-back: The Loafer

Loafers come in all shapes and sizes – some formal slip-ons, some tasselled and continental, some more casual still. Depending on style, colour, fabric and feel, the loafer can work for both smart and casual. Pair with tonally complementary socks – save loafing about sock-free for warm summer weekends.

## *Modern Twist: The Boot*

A classic leather Chelsea boot, with round toes, elastic sides and no laces, has echoes of The Beatles and works with a suit and jeans; suede Chelsea boots offer a more textured, casual feel. Chukka or desert boots, in suede or leather, are even more laid-back, perfect for jeans, chinos or a smart casual office.

---

### DON'T REPLACE, REPAIR: THE GOODYEAR WELT

Look out for shoes with a Goodyear welt, a special manufacturing method that allows for worn-out soles to be removed and replaced easily. A cork filler is added to the structure, which also increases comfort. Goodyear-welted shoes not only have a great lifespan but are also supportive, durable and waterproof. A wise, long-term investment.

---

## UMBRELLAS

~ Short, foldaways are the most practical but a long, curve-handled umbrella always looks elegant.

~ Golfing umbrellas are for the golf course or the great outdoors, but not the commute (unless you're keen to take someone's eye out).

# Coats

## PERFECT PARTNERS: OVERCOATS AND SUITS

~ Keep it simple and traditional with classic dark grey, navy or black.

~ Single-breasted allows you to wear it both done-up and undone. Buttoned-up, it should feel comfortably close but not tight.

~ Wear your suit when you go shopping for a coat. Check the coat shoulders sit right at the edge of your shoulders, and that the sleeves brush the top of your hand when your hand is bent out at a right angle to your wrist.

~ For wet weather, a blue or tan mac or trench coat does the job. It should be fitted rather than flapping about. (For informal coats, see p.124).

---

### ETIQUETTE SOS: HELPING WITH COATS

Keep it unfussy and slick: hold the coat open with one hand on each shoulder, allow the wearer to slip in their arms, give it a lift to help it into position and – this is the bit most people don't know – lift gently one more time to help it settle comfortably.

## STYLE IT OUT: HOW TO TIE A SCARF

*A good scarf can be a flourish, a dash of colour on a dreary day. Don't just let it hang - try your hand with one of these instead ...*

### The Drape

*How to:* Place the scarf around your neck with the loose ends at equal lengths. Put on your coat or jacket, and smoothly tuck the ends under the lapel on each side.

*Best with a smart coat or suit jacket as your shirt and tie stay on show.*

### The Wrap

*How to:* Place the scarf around your neck, with one end hanging down twice as long as the other. Wrap the longer end around your neck. Leave the ends loose, or tuck into the loop or lapels.

*Simple but adds detail to your overall look. Keep it slightly loose - don't over-tighten.*

### The Loop

*How to:* Fold the scarf in half lengthways. Place, folded, around your neck and thread the loose ends through the folded-end loop. Tighten and adjust - add formality by smoothing and straightening the folded loop after tying.

*The warmest and most stylish of them all. Simple as that.*

# Formalities

———◆◆———◆◆———◆◆———

### FORMAL DRESS CODES

•

### BIRTHS, WEDDINGS AND DEATHS

•

### FORMAL EVENTS

'IT IS NICE TO BE PART OF THE
CONVERSATION – JUST BE
SURE THEY ARE TALKING ABOUT
YOU IN THE RIGHT WAY.'

DAMIAN LEWIS

# Watch and Learn

It's easy to get daunted by decorum, but standing on ceremony and adopting faux formalities won't make you look smart and sophisticated. When you're stepping out in your best bib and tucker – black tie at a work dinner, morning dress at a wedding, your best suit for a swanky drinks party – look at ease and you'll look like know what you are doing.

If you feel like an amateur, don't show or tell. The most cunning plan is to watch and learn from those who truly know – recognising the clues, noticing the nuances, reading social codes and embracing the rituals are all part of learning the ropes. Confidence comes with experience: you can bend the rules once you truly understand them, but it never looks good to completely break them.

# Formal Dress Codes

~~~~~~~~~~~~~~~~~~~~~~~~~~~~~~~~~~~~~~~~~~~~~~~~~~~~~~~~~~~~~~~~

## PLAY BY THE RULES: WHY DRESS CODES MATTER

~ Dress codes simplify life by instructing you what to wear –
enjoy doing what you are told for once.

~ Wearing the same thing as everyone else levels the playing
field, and helps you ease into the formalities without feeling
too self-conscious.

~ Fashionable or artistic interpretations of the classics make
you look ignorant, not inspiring.

~ Embrace the pomp. What else are you going to do:
takeaway and TV, a pint down the local? Dust off your
dinner jacket and enjoy.

~~~~~~~~~~~~~~~~~~~~~~~~~~~~~~~~~~~~~~~~~~~~~~~~~~~~~~~~~~~~~~~~

## DRESS CODE: WHITE TIE

### The smartest of eveningwear

Most people never get to wear a white tie. Events this formal
are few and far between – royal ceremonies, state and livery
dinners, the smartest of Highland Balls – but, if you are lucky
enough to get an invitation to the Palace, step up and dress
up. Get it wrong and you'll have the great and the good quietly

sniggering at you as this mightiest of dress codes quickly exposes the in-the-knows from the don't-knows, so swot up and be battle-ready.

~ *Identify it*: Tailcoat and white bow tie.

~ *On the invitation*: 'White Tie', 'Full Evening Dress'.

~ *Also called*: 'Tails'.

## What to wear:

~ Black wool tailcoat with grosgrain silk peaked lapels, covered buttons and a single vent in the back. Knee-length and always worn undone.

(FYI) *Know your tailcoat from your morning coat. The clue is in the fronts: a morning coat continuously curves away from the lapel to the tail, whereas the tailcoat is distinctly cut away at the waist.*

~ Black high-waisted, pleated and tapered trousers with double braiding (side stripes of grosgrain silk on the outside leg seam). Can be worn with formal white braces.

~ White marcella waistcoat – double-breasted with a shawl collar is smartest. Sometimes backless.

(FYI) *This is the one and only occasion when you can get away with a backless waistcoat; tailcoats must be kept on all evening, and can be warm to wear, so going backless is a good idea if it's going to be hot.*

~ White marcella bib shirt with double cuffs and a wing collar (either part of the shirt, or a detachable one is fitted to a tunic collar with collar studs), worn with cufflinks and shirt studs. A loop on the yoke (the bit across the shoulders) keeps a backless waistcoat in place.

~ A white marcella bow tie (it's called 'white tie' for a reason) and always hand tied.

~ Patent black lace-up Oxford shoes (keep it plain and shiny, so no toecaps or broguing); black ribbon laces are traditional. Avoid opera pumps – dainty shoes with bows never suited any man.

~ Black socks, long enough to insure against any flashes of calf when seated. Black silk socks are luxurious and traditional but, in reality, slip down.

**White Tie Tips:**

~ White gloves and scarves look more Fred Astaire than *savoir faire*, so steer clear.

~ Part the tails, rather than moving them to one side, when sitting down in a tailcoat.

~ Top hats are rarely worn nowadays but, if you insist, they are never worn indoors.

## DISASTROUS DIPLOMATIC DRESSING

Frankenstein, Fred Flintstone and Batman's Penguin …
just some of the comparisons made to Donald Trump in
2019 when he wore ill-fitting white tie to the state dinner at
Buckingham Palace. As Melania shone in full-length white
(which, as many noted, was more *Dancing on Ice* than First
Lady), Trump's trousers fell inches too long, were cut inches
too wide and, at the waist, sat inches too low. His coat
sleeves and waistcoat were too long, but the body and
tails of the coat too short. Unsurprisingly, no tailor claimed
responsibility for (disastrously) dressing the president.

## ETIQUETTE SOS: DECORATIONS

Royal or state events can have a white tie dress code of
'Evening Dress – Decorations'. This means medals (not baubles)
and usually that a member of the Royal Family will be showing
up so, if you have any, wear them. Not relevant for most of us
but, if you have been decorated, don't do a Beckham – be sure
to wear them on the left side of your tailcoat.

## EYE FOR DETAIL: SHIRT STUDS

An essential for white tie and a classy detail for black tie, shirt
studs are little dumbbell-shaped fasteners. Evening shirts
feature an extra buttonhole to host the shirt studs, which are
pushed through from the back and sit on show at the front.

Go for a bold black onyx to coordinate with the bow tie, or a more subtle mother-of-pearl to match the shirt (usefully, they often come double-ended featuring both so you can choose). Never mix and match and avoid anything novelty or sparkly.

## DRESS CODE: BLACK TIE

### Smart eveningwear

It is highly likely that, if you haven't already, you will pull on a dinner jacket for a black tie event at some point. Whether it's a work do or a private party, black tie is the go-to dress code for special evening events (that is, correctly, after six o'clock). Yes, it's more of a faff than sticking on your usual suit, but who doesn't feel great and, let's just admit it, a little 007-like in a dinner jacket?

~ *Identify it*: Black bow tie – think James Bond.

~ *On the invitation*: 'Black Tie' (or in America 'Tuxedos').

~ *Also called*: 'Dinner Jackets', 'DJs'.

**FYI** *Call it a 'dinner suit' and you sound like Del Boy.*

### What to wear:

~ Black wool jacket with silk peaked lapels or a shawl collar, covered buttons and no vents. Can be single- or double-breasted. Single-breasted dinner jackets traditionally have only one button, which is not done up.

**FYI** *Dinner jackets are never taken off.*

~ Black, slightly tapered, trousers with a single line of braiding (side stripes of grosgrain silk on the outside leg seam).

~ White marcella evening shirt, fastened either with buttons or studs. Alternatives include covered buttons or vertical front pleats. Always double cuffs (and cufflinks) and a turn-down collar.

🔵 *Wing collars should never be worn for black tie.*

~ Black bow tie – always hand tied (see below). Never wear a black tie instead of a bow tie – it even looks wrong in Hollywood.

~ Black highly polished (or patent) lace-up shoes; long black socks.

~ Pocket squares should be white silk.

## Black Tie Tips:

~ Never wear a pre-tied bow tie – it marks you as an uninformed amateur from a mile off and is equivalent to wearing a cardigan with a shirt front sewn inside.

~ White dinner jackets are a thing of the tropics and cruise ships and will make you look like you're at the captain's cocktail party or the dinner dance at the all-inclusive.

~ Velvet smoking jackets can be worn for black tie in certain situations (see p.59).

**JAMES BOND:** I HAVE A
DINNER JACKET.

**VESPER LYND:** THERE ARE
DINNER JACKETS AND DINNER
JACKETS; THIS IS THE LATTER.
AND I NEED YOU LOOKING
LIKE A MAN WHO BELONGS
AT THAT TABLE.

*CASINO ROYALE*

## CUMMERBUNDS

Cummerbunds are not incorrect, they just feel a bit 1980s.
If you must, then wear with the pleats facing up. Why? First,
because of tradition as the pleats used to be used instead of a
pocket for theatre/opera tickets. Second, for a practical reason –
cummerbunds have the nickname of 'crumb catchers' because
the upwards-facing pleats do just that when you break your
bread roll at the dinner table.

## HOW THE DINNER JACKET KILLED THE TAILCOAT

Back when dressing for dinner meant wearing a tailcoat every evening, the future King Edward VII (then Prince of Wales) wanted to wear something more comfortable. In 1865 his tailor, Henry Poole, designed a short, ventless jacket in blue; he got rid of the tails, but kept it suitably smart by retaining the formal lapels. It was popular with the trend-setting prince and was soon adopted by his high-society set.

Soon after, Edward hosted influential American millionaire James Brown Potter and his wife at Sandringham. Unsure of what to wear when staying with a British prince, Brown Potter visited Henry Poole who recommended this new style of dinner jacket. Back in New York, Brown Potter wore it to a private country club in Tuxedo Park, and this new trend, endorsed by British royalty, became an instant hit with New York society – and was named the 'tuxedo'.

But it took much longer for the more traditional British establishment to accept such an informal style for evening dress. The Second World War changed things as tailcoats were seen as too flashy and inappropriate in a time of austerity and, in 1940, the British papers reported King George VI dining in a dinner jacket rather than a tailcoat. With the dinner jacket now the 'ruling fashion', white tie and tailcoats were banished and, like now, only worn at the most formal events.

## HOST WITH THE MOST: VELVET SLIPPERS

Velvet slippers, paired with a matching velvet smoking jacket, are traditionally worn by a host to offer him some comfort when entertaining at home in black tie. Known as 'Albert slippers' after Prince Albert popularised them as a clean house shoe to wear in the Palace, they have connotations of confidence, wealth and power. Winston Churchill was a fan, and Hugh Hefner slipped them on, along with a smoking jacket, for special evenings at the Playboy Mansion.

Recently, however, velvet slippers have crept out of private homes and onto the red carpet, seen on both Hollywood stars and young British princes. If you are keeping open-minded company and are exceptionally confident you can pull it off, then velvet slippers might just be for you – but keep it plain, black and monogram-free.

'I THINK I HAVE SOMETHING TONIGHT
THAT'S NOT QUITE CORRECT FOR
EVENING WEAR. BLUE SUEDE SHOES.'

**ELVIS PRESLEY**

## DRESS CODE: MORNING DRESS

*Formal daywear*

When it comes to dressing up in the daytime (so, correctly, for events before six o'clock), 'morning dress' is the smartest of dress codes. Traditionally it is what men wear for British weddings, as well as some official functions (e.g. garden parties at the Palace) and society events (e.g. Royal Ascot). It's the quintessential British gent's garb – driven by tradition but with a touch of peacock and panache.

~ *Identify it*: Long morning coat (jacket).

~ *On the invitation*: 'Morning Dress' (but not usually included on wedding invitations, even though it is the traditional dress code).

~ *Also called*: 'Formal Day Dress'.

(FYI) *Call it a 'Morning Suit' and you sound like a bookie.*

**What to wear:**

~ Black or grey single-breasted morning coat (jacket) with a curved front and tails.

~ Grey or pinstriped-grey trousers – don't worry, it's correct that they don't match the coat (jacket).

~ White or pale pastel shirt, with a turn-down collar and proper tie.

> 🔘 *Never go for a wing collar with cravat and stickpin – it says hire shop, not high society.*

~ Single- or double-breasted waistcoat, preferably with lapels; grey, sandy or duck-egg colours look the smartest.

~ Smart, preferably lace-up, shoes (never patent).

> 🔘 *Loafers are too casual and, strictly speaking, brogues a bit too business-y.*

**Morning Dress Tips:**

~ There is usually a loop behind the buttonhole on the left to secure a boutonnière.

~ Black or grey top hats are required for the races (e.g. Royal Ascot), but optional at weddings (and often a pain to look after all day so best left).

~ A pocket square can add a splash of colour and personality (see p.31).

## CUFFLINK RULES

The key thing to remember with cufflinks is that they are useful first, and a statement second. They should be functional by design, but impressive as if by chance – the rule of thumb is expensive, but discreet. So, eschew novelty, avoid bling and keep them classy.

Always wear a pair – never mix and match – and it can be nice to match watch and cufflink metals. For white tie, they should be pearl or silver only, but onyx, silver, gold and mother-of-pearl are great with black tie.

**FYI** *Keep a pair of fabric, knot cufflinks in your washbag for emergency use. You will inevitably, at some stage, forget your proper cufflinks and these are a perfectly acceptable life-saver in a pinch – and for under a fiver too.*

## DRESS CODE: LOUNGE SUIT

### Smart daytime or eveningwear

The occasions when you need to stick on a suit – daytime and evening business events; formal occasions, such as smart lunches; drinks receptions and dinners – are given the dress code 'Lounge Suit'. Striking fear into many that their ordinary business suit won't cut the mustard, it is just arcane terminology to tell you that you must wear a suit and that you may just wear your go-to suit.

**FYI** *You normally need to wear a tie too.*

~ *Identify it*: Business or occasion suit.

~ *On the invitation*: 'Lounge Suit'.

~ *Also called*: 'Business Dress', 'Business Attire'.

~ *What to wear*: see The Suit, p.11.

---

**A NOTE ON SUNGLASSES**

You're not in *La Dolce Vita*. Even if faced with the sunniest of skies, never put on your shades when wearing a suit or morning dress at a formal event or you quickly morph from British gent to clichéd salesman.

---

## STYLE IT OUT: SMOKING JACKETS

~ Originally worn by men when smoking as the velvet caught the smell and any ash. Think port and cigars.

~ Can be worn (by the brave) in blue, burgundy or dark green as a black tie alternative to the dinner jacket, paired with black tie trousers, shirt and bow tie (and, if you want to go the whole hog, matching velvet slippers).

~ Strictly only the host can wear this in his own home - guests should wear normal black tie.

~ Young aristos have been known to wear smoking jackets with jeans at home to dress down to dress up. Could look a bit unusual in a suburban semi-detached.

·•——••——••·

'ONLY TWO RULES REALLY COUNT.
NEVER MISS AN OPPORTUNITY TO
RELIEVE YOURSELF; NEVER MISS
A CHANCE TO SIT DOWN AND
REST YOUR FEET.'

**EDWARD VIII**

·•——••——••·

# Births, Weddings and Deaths

## Births

*Best behaviour for when someone has a baby …*

**Rule 1:** Hop to it. Whether you get a personal text message or see the news on social media, an enthusiastic and speedy reply/like/comment is your first duty. If you have seen a photo, try something meaningful like, 'She looks beautiful – I can't wait to meet her', rather than 'Cute kid'. Even though most newborn babies look a bit like E.T., the parents will be overcome by its beauty (and will claim non-existent family resemblances).

**Rule 2:** Drop a line. Pop a card in the post but, in case there are complications, hold off until everyone is back home. Address it to the parents, not the baby; bonus points if you include the baby's name in your message (double-check that social media announcement to avoid any gaffes).

**Rule 3:** Present and correct. You should buy a gift for a close friend's baby. Good options include soft toys, check the label to see if it's safe for newborns; a baby blanket; clothes, go for a size up (e.g. 3–6 months and on a season so it's suitable for the weather when it fits) or something for the nursery like a small framed print, wall clock or mobile.

**Rule 4:** Call of duty. Leave it a while before visiting, and never show up uninvited. Take a present not only for the baby, but also something small for any other siblings (e.g. a toy or book for a toddler) and something nice for the mother (after all, she did most of the hard work). Be prepared to go with the flow and if you know them well, offer to stick the kettle on. Don't outstay your welcome.

**Rule 5:** Baby brain. New parents are sometimes a shadow of their former selves. If you haven't had kids of your own, it can seem like your best mate is a changed man. Prepare yourself: things will be unequivocally baby-focused; breast-feeding and nappy-talk will be normal parlance. Even the most alpha male of men coo, stare and think they saw it smile (it's probably wind, but keep quiet). Who said change doesn't happen overnight? With new parents, it really does.

'HAVING CHILDREN IS LIKE LIVING
IN A FRAT HOUSE: NOBODY SLEEPS,
EVERYTHING'S BROKEN AND THERE'S
A LOT OF THROWING UP.'

**RAY ROMANO**

## LIFE ROLES: THE GODPARENT

It is an honour to be asked to be a godparent. You will have been discussed at great length and been deemed a good influence, reliable and thoughtful, as well as generous. Well done you: now you have to live up to your reputation and do a good job.

**Go one better.** The christening present is the chance to shine against the godparenting competition. Hallmarked tankards, rattles and spoons will tarnish at the back of the cupboard, so go for something more practical. A money or jewellery box, a collection of books (Roald Dahl, Harry Potter, Beatrix Potter), a limited-edition classic teddy bear. If you want to push the boat out, buy some wine in bond to be released when your godchild turns 18 or 21, but seek advice from a decent wine merchant on suitable vintages and storage practicalities.

**One to remember.** Never forget a birthday, give something at Christmas – stick your hand in your pocket and be generous. When they are small, it's really about showing the parents that you are the godfather they cracked you up to be. When they are older, go for slightly unsuitable presents – this will curry favour and give you some recognition if you don't see them very often.

**Pen friend.** When they are younger, send postcards from your holidays. When they are older, a good luck card or message for exams and tests. Remember milestones – new schools, confirmations, driving tests, graduations, engagements …

**Good turns.** When they are older, help them out. Swap presents with cash for birthdays and Christmas. Let them access your network – make introductions for hard-to-find internships and help them on their professional journey.

**As good as your word.** Stick around. Don't be the godparent that disappears; even if your friendship with the parents fades, be sure to maintain contact with your godchild. A successful godfather keeps his role for life in some shape or form, not just until they are confirmed or 18.

~~~~~~~~~~~~~~~~~~~~~~~~~~~~~~~~~~~~~~~~~~~~~~~

## IN THE KNOW: CHRISTENINGS

~   Christenings – also called baptisms – may take place during an ordinary Sunday church service or may be a private service.

~   Dress smart: wear a suit and, if chilly, make sure your coat is up to scratch.

~   Take a present with you. Godparents should be generous; ordinary guests don't need to break the bank.

~ If you are a godparent, then you need to prove your mettle. You will be called up to the front during the service, and you may have to hold the baby. Afterwards, you should circulate and socialise, acknowledge the baby again, and don't be the first to leave.

~ There is usually food and drink afterwards, either in a venue or at the family's home. It's normally a small affair, and you aren't expected to stick around for hours, especially if it's informal buffet-style, rather than a sit-down lunch. There will be a toast and possibly a short speech.

~ Non-religious couples may go for a naming ceremony. This can be an informal get-together, such as a lunch, or may be more formalised with an 'official' celebrant. Check the invitation to see how smart things are and what you should wear. Take a present; the baby might not notice if you don't, but the parents certainly will.

# Weddings

## ETIQUETTE SOS: ENGAGEMENTS

*What to do when someone (else) pops the question ...*

**Rule 1:** Even if you think your best mate has just signed himself up for a life of misery, be suitably thrilled and suggest a congratulatory drink. For distant friends and friends-of-friends, a congratulatory comment on social media or a quick text message is fine.

**Rule 2:** Send an engagement card. Your mum may have told you to never send one jointly to the couple, but nowadays it's fine (traditionally cards were sent separately; congratulatory ones to the groom-to-be, but good wishes to the bride-to-be – she was never congratulated as it implied surprise that she'd 'caught' a man who would take her on ...).

**Rule 3:** Give close friends a present (champagne, a decent bottle of wine), send flowers, or get together and treat them to a meal. Be prepared for recollections of the engagement, flashes of the ring and wedding-day chatter. Reassure yourself that once the realities of wedding planning sets in – budgets, tricky step-parents, seating plans – your mate will be on the phone begging for a wedding-free pint.

**Rule 4:** If there is a proper engagement party hosted by the couple, take a present (if you haven't already given them anything). Afterwards, thank them for the party; traditionalists or older hosts (e.g. the couple's parents) by post, otherwise a text or email is fine. You should assume you will get a wedding invitation if you have been invited to the engagement party – as long as you haven't shocked the mother-of-the-bride or upset a bridesmaid.

•————••————•

'SHE'S A WONDERFUL,
WONDERFUL PERSON, AND WE'RE
LOOKING TO A HAPPY AND
WONDERFUL NIGHT – AH, LIFE.'

**EDWARD KENNEDY**

•————••————•

---

## DIAMONDS: AN ADVERTISING DREAM

Should you spend two months' salary on an engagement ring? It's been the 'going rate' for decades, assumed to be an age-old gentleman's agreement lurking in the murky waters of engagement etiquette – along with asking her father and getting down on one knee. But it is a *Mad Men*-esque concept that has resonated for decades, all stemming from a simple phrase that would have caught Don Draper's eye.

With diamonds falling from favour after the Great Depression, De Beers needed something to rejuvenate and reposition the image of the diamond in America. In the mid 1940s, a young female copywriter at a Philadelphia ad agency, N.W. Ayer & Son, coined the phrase 'A diamond is forever' – a simple slogan that is still used by De Beers today.

Diamonds quickly became associated with 'indestructible love', along with a direct correlation of wealth and size of stone. De Beers furthered this idea in the 1970s when their landmark TV ad asked, 'How else could two months' salary last forever? A diamond is forever' – and the myth of the 'correct' price of an engagement ring was born.

## ETIQUETTE SOS: WEDDING GUESTS

*Be the best wedding guest ...*

**Rule 1:** Never assume you have a 'plus 1'. Only those named on the invitation are invited, or it will clearly say 'and guest'. Asking to bring your new partner puts the hosts on the spot and opens the floodgates if they agree, and they don't want their wedding photos full of people they've never met.

**Rule 2:** Buy a gift (or not). Most of the time, wedding lists are a simple go-online-and-choose scenario; others may ask for money (which is fine nowadays). Some may request no presents at all, but do be generous in another way – take them out or ask them over after the honeymoon.

**Rule 3:** Dress the part. Dress codes are not included on a wedding invitation when it is traditional, so it's safe to assume morning dress or a lounge suit is appropriate (see p.56 and p.58). Watch out for couples trying to create a day with a difference – dinner jackets for evening receptions, or even dress codes with a colour theme (you can blame the social media influencers for this).

**Rule 4:** On form. Wedding fatigue can quickly hit if you find yourself travelling to a different corner of the country every weekend, watching another couple tie the knot. It's just a phase that comes with age – dig deep and be on your best form. Don't be late; don't complain; don't change the seating plan; don't get shamefully legless.

'IF I'M THE BEST MAN,
WHY IS SHE MARRYING HIM?'

**JERRY SEINFELD**

## LIFE ROLES: THE BEST MAN

Being a best man requires commitment, diplomacy, reliability, confidence, patience, tolerance, organisation and humour. And it helps if you remember the rings – and get on with the bride.

Really, it's a matter of nailing the three big tasks: the stag do, the wedding-day duties and the speech.

### Task 1: The Stag Do

~   It's in your interest to encourage the groom to keep it small – it makes everything easier to organise.

~   A 'pre-stag' is a thing – it's a dinner or drinks a few weeks beforehand so as many of the group as possible can meet. Only for the very (overly?) committed.

~   Keep it affordable for the whole group (and be clear about costs from the start). It's a nice touch for everyone to cover some or all of the groom's costs.

~   Tailor the stag do to the groom – don't feel afraid of a quiet one for a quieter guy, or a big one for someone more exuberant.

~   Wall-to-wall weekend boozing never turns out well. Plan drink-free activities; book lunch and dinners to ensure everyone eats.

~   Don't force everyone to wear fancy dress, go to a strip club or act crazy. Pre-planned humiliation and public shame is never as funny as it sounds.

~   Don't overshare on social media and use the ultimate filter: if it was a photo of you, would you be happy?

## *Task 2: Wedding-Day Duties*

~ Meet the VIPs – the couple's parents, the bridesmaids, etc. Watch out for potential dramas – divorced parents, ex-lovers, warring cousins, staunch enemies …

~ Know what is happening and when, from the ceremony timings to the order of play at the reception.

~ Tell the photographer who you are. You might be needed to gather groups for family photos, or to make sure they snap the big moments – e.g. cutting the cake, first dance, etc.

~ Get the groom to the church on time. That's really important.

~ Don't leave the ushers to it – it's an easy role to slack off from, but a really helpful one if done right.

~ Handing over the rings is (one of) your big moments. Don't forget them.

~ No knocking off early – you need to be the last man standing.

~ Duties may also include talking to mad relatives; making sure the wedding presents don't get nicked; telling the DJ to up his game; making sure people dance to hard-to-dance-to music; rounding up drunk cougar aunts. You've been warned.

### Task 3: Speech Success

~ Prepare properly. You should know it well enough that if you are sent off-piste or lose your place, you can get back on track easily.

~ Grab your audience's attention from the get-go. And don't forget about a killer ending – if the running order is traditional, you will be the closing act.

~ Make sure you are both seen and heard. Strike a good pose by standing up tall, with your shoulders down and back. Don't forget about a bit of eye contact with your listeners too.

~ You're obviously a VIP in the groom's life, so act up. Don't be afraid of a little heartfelt emotion.

~ Never ever, ever, ever get gags off the internet. Everyone has heard them all before, really.

~ Don't rush. Go slowly, and then go even slower. You may want it over with, but the audience want to have time to hear what you are saying.

~ At the very least you can memorise the first and last line, and a couple in between. Don't stand up and read off an A4 printout; if you need it in front of you, use A5 cards.

~ Avoid unearthing best-forgotten truths or dropping bombs that may explode later. Remember, for every raucous friend of the groom, there is likely also a stale great aunt.

~ Get drunk after it, not before.

'LADIES AND GENTLEMEN ... THIS IS ONLY
THE SECOND TIME I'VE BEEN A BEST MAN.
I HOPE I DID OK THAT TIME. THE COUPLE
IN QUESTION ARE AT LEAST STILL TALKING
TO ME. UNFORTUNATELY, THEY'RE NOT
ACTUALLY TALKING TO EACH OTHER.
THE DIVORCE CAME THROUGH A COUPLE
OF MONTHS AGO. BUT I'M ASSURED IT
HAD ABSOLUTELY NOTHING TO DO WITH
ME. PAULA KNEW PIERS HAD SLEPT WITH
HER SISTER BEFORE I MENTIONED IT IN
THE SPEECH. THE FACT THAT HE'D SLEPT
WITH HER MOTHER CAME AS A SURPRISE,
BUT I THINK WAS INCIDENTAL TO THE
NIGHTMARE OF RECRIMINATION AND
VIOLENCE THAT BECAME THEIR
TWO-DAY MARRIAGE.'

**CHARLES,** *FOUR WEDDINGS AND A FUNERAL*

# Deaths

*Do the right thing when someone dies.*

**Rule 1:** Send a handwritten letter of condolence to the family. Don't be over-familiar or too emotional; and don't presume to know how they are feeling or use overly theatrical language. Keep it brief and focus on fond memories and good anecdotes. If you are short on literary skills, or if you didn't know them very well, a card might be easier.

**Rule 2:** For younger people and less formal families, send an email or text message; for the closest friends, speak on the phone or offer to visit. Be cautious of only relying on the social media bandwagon; posts about tragedy often just attract a barrage of insincere comments by lesser-known friends and followers, so while you should 'like' any posts, be sure to get in touch directly.

**Rule 3:** The request of 'family flowers only' should be respected and often a charitable donation made instead. If you know the family well and want to do more than just write a letter, then by all means send flowers to the family privately – a good idea if you cannot attend the funeral.

## IN THE KNOW: FUNERALS

~ Wear a dark suit and a black or sombre tie and, in winter, a formal coat.

~ Arrive in good time. If you are late, wait outside until the end rather than creeping in during the service.

~ The front rows will be for family and VIPs. If you have small children or a baby with you, sit near the back on the end of a row for an easy exit in case of a behavioural emergency.

~ Stand up when the family enters the church or crematorium, and also for any hymns. Even if you are a non-believer, be still during prayers.

~ After the service or at the wake, the family may form a line-up to greet guests and thank them for coming. If necessary, introduce yourself and tell them how you fit in (just your name isn't very helpful). Avoid clichés or overly emotional remarks.

~ Dress is the same for memorial services; they are similar to funerals but may be more upbeat as usually a few months will have passed since the death.

———— ✦ ✦ ————

'PEOPLE'S NUMBER ONE FEAR
IS PUBLIC SPEAKING. NUMBER TWO IS
DEATH ... THIS MEANS TO THE AVERAGE
PERSON, IF YOU HAVE TO GO TO A
FUNERAL, YOU'RE BETTER OFF IN THE
CASKET THAN DOING THE EULOGY.'

**JERRY SEINFELD**

———— ✦ ✦ ————

# Formal Events

## THE SMARTEST OF THEM ALL: ROYAL OCCASIONS

### *Garden Parties*

~ If you get the chance to go, enjoy it as, officially, once you've been once, you can't go again.

~ The dress code is morning dress, or lounge suits. Given it's a one-off, and you may meet members of the Royal Family, try to wear morning dress.

~ Gates open at three o'clock; the Royals arrive at four o'clock – you won't miss it, as the military band plays the National Anthem.

~ Scoff as much of the afternoon tea as you like (but remember your manners – you are at the Palace).

~ On that note, you can wander the grounds – which at 39 acres is the largest private garden in London.

## ROYAL TACKLE

Dropping his trousers, shouting 'wa-hey' and running across the Palace lawns towards the Queen, a 17-year-old wannabe streaker caused a stir at a garden party in 2003. A Yeoman of the Guard manning the gate of the royal tea tent came to the rescue by rugby-tackling the rebel to the ground, luckily while he still had his boxers on. The Queen remained characteristically unshaken, coolly remarking, 'Oh dear'. It was probably worse for the flashing youth's red-faced parents and brother who were also there – family chat on the train home must have been a touch awkward.

'I HOPE YOU'RE NOT GOING TO SPOIL THINGS WITH LOWER MIDDLE-CLASS HUMOUR.'

**HYACINTH BUCKET,** *KEEPING UP APPEARANCES*

## STATE BANQUETS

~ The ticket money can't buy. The invitation is a command from the sovereign, and there are very few excuses that allow you to refuse. Planning starts over a year in advance.

~ The dress code is 'White Tie' – and White Tie only. Even your bespoke dinner jacket won't cut it.

~ On arrival, guests congregate in the drawing rooms, before being presented to the sovereign and then finding their seats (with the help of an enormous seating plan) for dinner in the ballroom.

~ Everything is led by the sovereign. Sit when they sit, eat when they eat, finish when they finish (even if there is still food on your plate).

~ Be prepared for toasts and speeches before the meal, not afterwards as you may be used to.

~ You'll be eating off china from King George IV's 4,000-piece dinner set that took eight weeks to unpack. The table takes five days to set and over 1,000 glasses will be used. That's a lot of tissue paper and tea towels.

~ It's all done and dusted in 80 minutes. Twelve pipers play and walk around the room, clearly telling everyone it's time to call an Uber – but wait until you're outside, no phones in the Palace please.

---

### STATE SICKNESS

Tokyo, 1992, and George H.W. Bush was on a state visit to Japan. He had felt unwell after a tense game of tennis doubles against the emperor of Japan, but the president ignored doctor's advice and attended the state dinner. His bold decision backfired: during the meal, Bush vomited on Kiichi Miyazawa, the Japanese prime minister. As the First Lady, the Secret Service and his private physician came swiftly to his aid, Bush is said to have uttered, 'Roll me under the table until the dinner's over'.

## ETIQUETTE SOS: FORMAL EVENTS

**What to wear?** Check the invitation; if there's a dress code, it will be on it. Expect 'black tie' or 'lounge suit' for most events – 'white tie' is rare (see p.47).

**When to arrive?** In Britain, you don't need to be bang on time, but mustn't be properly late, and never, ever early. Confused? If the invitation says '7 o'clock for 7.30pm' or '7 o'clock for dinner' then arrive by 7.10pm.

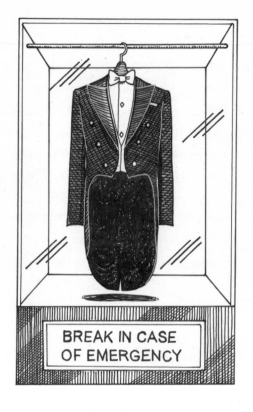

BREAK IN CASE
OF EMERGENCY

Drinks are more relaxed, so for '7 o'clock drinks', you can pitch up between 7.10-7.20pm.

**A drinks party?** It is what it says on the tin. Standing, having a drink and a chat, and usually a canapé or two. You can be casually late (see above) and there is often no official end time, but two hours is a usual length for the whole event (e.g. 7-9pm). Say hello to your host when you arrive; try to say goodbye, but if it's very busy then it's fine to slip away unnoticed.

**A formal dinner?** Arrival drinks are followed by a sit-down dinner. Find your name on the seating plan and then your place at the table (and no swapping of place cards, even if you've landed the worst company). Wait for other people to arrive at your table before sitting down. At very formal events, stay standing for grace (and sometimes the National Anthem). Food is then served (usually three to four courses), top table manners apply and sparkling conversation is a must. There may be toasts and speeches after the meal. The end, often referred to as 'Carriages' on the invitation, is usually obvious and punctual.

**And afterwards?** It's good form to put pen to paper and thank the hosts after a lavish, formal event. For business and less formal occasions, a well-written email will do.

## IN THE KNOW: INVITATIONS DECODED

~   Look at the RSVP on the invitation to know how to reply –
    e.g. a postal address needs a handwritten posted reply and
    an email address an email reply.

~   Be quick to reply – within a few days, rather than a few
    weeks. Don't be a straggler, or worse, find yourself on the
    host's chase-up list. If there is a reply card enclosed, use it.

~   Formal invitations require a formally worded reply, and
    there is a traditional formula (if you cannot make it, you
    don't need to give a reason why unless you know the host
    well – when you would send a separate note explaining):

### For formal events:

*Mr James Anderson thanks The Charity for their kind invitation for Saturday, 20th January, which he has much pleasure in accepting / regrets he is unable to accept.*

### For formal wedding invitations:

*Mr James Anderson thanks Mr and Mrs Charles Tyrwhitt for the kind invitation to the marriage of their daughter, Camilla, to Mr Tom Smith at St Laurence's Church, Ludlow, on Saturday, 20th January at 3 o'clock and afterwards at The Manor House, and are delighted to accept / regret they are unable to accept.*

Use the invitation to give you some clues about the event. Helpfully, there are some assumptions you can make:

~ The more formal the invitation, the more formal the event.

~ Evening events are generally smarter than daytime events.

~ City events will usually be more contemporary and formal than country/rural events.

~ The choice of venue will give you an idea of style and tone.

~ Annual events will have hashtags/pictures on social media from previous years to give you an idea of what to expect.

~ The hosts influence the style and tone - e.g. are they young or old? Traditional or contemporary? Have you been to one of their parties before?

# Grooming

◆◆———————◆———————◆◆

**SHAVING • BEARDS**
**HAIR • SKINCARE**
**SMELING GOOD**
**TREATMENTS • SLEEP**

'EVERY MAN SHOULD HAVE
A MAGNIFYING MIRROR.
IF YOU LOOK GOOD MAGNIFIED,
YOU ARE SET TO GO.'

**TOM FORD**

# Keep up the Routine

Ever noticed how some people don't shave for a few days and look great, while others just look hungover? The key to looking rugged rather than rough is a simple grooming regime – and it doesn't take much effort. Learn to shave properly and invest in a decent haircut. Keep nails clean and trimmed, eyebrows as two separate entities and nose and ear hair absent. Moisturise, exfoliate, wear a cologne. And, most important, keep teeth and mouth clean – a good smile gets you anywhere and one thing pandemic face masks should have taught you is the effect of bad breath.

# Shaving

### Weekday Wet Shave (time-short)

1. Run your hands over your stubble and see which way it grows (hint: lots of different directions).

2. Run hot water and splash over your face.

3. Apply shaving foam or cream (moisturiser can be a good alternative for those with sensitive skin), ideally with a brush to stand your stubble upright.

4. Shave with the direction of hair growth.

5. Rinse with very cold water.

### Weekend Wet Shave (time-rich)

1. Again, work out in which direction your stubble grows.

2. Fill a bowl with boiling water, drape a towel over your head and shoulders, then hover over the bowl for ten minutes to allow the steam to open your pores fully.

3. Apply shaving cream in a firm, circular motion to stand your stubble upright.

4. Shave with the direction of hair growth.

5. Rinse your face with hot water.

6. Reapply shaving cream.

7. Shave again, this time against the direction of hair growth.

8. Rinse with very cold water to close the pores.

9. Moisturise immediately – and consider a menthol, cooling aftershave.

10. An alum block is cheap and very good for sore skin post-shave, while a styptic pencil will promptly seal any nicks.

---

'A GOOD LATHER
IS HALF THE SHAVE.'

**WILLIAM HONE**

---

## SMOOTH MOVE: RAZOR CHOICE

### *Disposable*

*Pros:* Cheap, available everywhere, useful when travelling.

*Cons:* A poor shave, hard to apply correct pressure to face when shaving, flimsy, poor-quality razor, environmentally unfriendly.

### Cartridge Razor

*Pros:* Simple to use, highly effective, very safe, flexible to follow the contours of the face.

*Cons:* Ridiculously costly (though new brands are taking on the big brands here) and short-lived. Each cartridge is generally effective for about five shaves, making them neither financially nor environmentally friendly.

### Safety Razor

*Pros:* An ultra-close shave, extremely cheap and long-lasting blades, the razor handle itself can last a lifetime, while their weight means less pressure is needed so razor-rash is less common. Also, frankly, the process of unscrewing, replacing the blade, then reassembling the razor makes you feel a bit like James Bond putting a pistol together.

*Cons:* Takes mastering. Nicks and cuts are commonplace early on. Initial outlay is much more than for a cartridge razor (though that investment evens out over time due to the cheapness of the razor blades).

### Electric

*Pros:* Versatile, quick, can be used anywhere, less messy and can be used with water and shaving cream.

*Cons:* Nowhere near as close a shave as a razor, bulky in the washbag, can leave skin irritated, expensive.

### Cut-throat

*Pros:* An ultra-close shave, feels quite macho, always quite cool handling a knife (though a little tricksy in a wet environment).

*Cons:* Pretty easy to cut your throat and bleed to death – best left to professionals, really.

•——•——•

'I CAN GUARANTEE THE CLOSEST
SHAVE YOU'LL EVER KNOW.'

**SWEENEY TODD,** *SWEENEY TODD:*
*THE DEMON BARBER OF FLEET STREET*

•——•——•

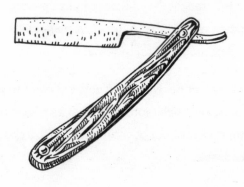

# Beards

## FIVE BEARD RULES

~ When growing a beard, resist the urge to shape it for a couple of weeks to allow it to thicken up. Then use a beard trimmer or clippers to keep it neat.

~ Keep the neck clean. Hold a finger just above the Adam's apple, point it towards your earlobe and shave anything under that (avoid going higher as you'll end up with a chin-strap beard); draw an imaginary line between the top of the ear and the corner of the mouth and shave anything above that.

~ For shorter beards, trim the sideburns, moustache, top of the neck and cheek to the same length (but leaving the hair on and just below the chin a touch longer can add shape).

~ For a long beard, trim in a downwards motion from the jawline to thin out straggling hairs but maintain length, then blend in the sideburns and moustache. Try not to let it get too wolfman – hillbilly can be a tough look to pull off in pay review meetings.

~ For goatees, soul patch beards, etc. apply a good-quality shaving cream to the beard in a circular motion, then reach for a fresh razor and shave thoroughly until the beard has entirely disappeared. You're welcome.

---

MR. TEAVEE: 'WHO WANTS A BEARD?'

WILLY WONKA: 'WELL, BEATNIKS FOR ONE, FOLK SINGERS, AND MOTORBIKE RIDERS ... ALL THOSE HIP, JAZZY, SUPER COOL, NEAT, KEEN, AND GROOVY CATS.'

**CHARLIE AND THE CHOCOLATE FACTORY**

---

## ESSENTIAL MAINTENANCE

**Lather up:** Beardruff and beard odour are very real problems, so use a proper beard shampoo that cleans and moisturises in all the right places (ordinary shampoo is too harsh and drying).

**Steam up:** Every now and again, apply hot flannels or steam your face over a bowl of boiling water. This allows the pores to open and helps cleanse the skin.

**Grease up:** Keep things in good condition with a beard oil. Squeeze two to three drops into your hand, rub between your palms and then apply by rubbing up and down the side of the face, under the chin (forward and back) and use a thumb and forefinger to work into the tache. Finally, use a comb to work through and style, and if you want a little more shine, finish with a balm.

**Brush up:** A beard brush keeps beards of all lengths clean and tidy (and dislodges those trapped morsels from your lunch). Beard combs are best used to detangle longer beards.

---

### BEARD DUTY

Beards used to be a costly business. Following travels around Europe and being struck by the clean-shaven faces of his successful European neighbours, in 1698 Peter the Great imposed a ban on beards in Russia. His directive was met with great resistance, particularly from the Russian Orthodox church, so he compromised by imposing a beard tax. When you paid up, you were given a small token - a bit like a coin - to prove you had hairy privileges if questioned.

# Hair

## A CUT ABOVE: HAIRCUTS

You slide on your £1,000 suit, £100 shirt and £80 silk tie. You lace up your £200 shoes and strap on your £2,000 watch. It's a big day, and you need to look good. A tweak of the pocket square, a dab of cologne and a last check in the mirror … but somehow you are still more Donald Trump than Donald Draper.

Which is when, hopefully, you realise that spending £15 on a haircut from a bloke with a set of rusty clippers, dubious personal hygiene and suspect banter is the biggest style mistake you will ever make. Your haircut is the one thing you wear with every outfit: you take it to work and out with your mates, you wear it on dates, to the supermarket and in the gym. It is the only thing that goes with everything in your wardrobe – and you're happy to leave that to a guy who thinks naming his shop The Mane Event or Hairforce One is pretty sharp? Think again.

Investing in a good haircut every five weeks or so is the single easiest way to upgrade your style game. It'll cost you about £300–500 a year – significantly less than, say, a new suit and a few work shirts – and will have twice the impact.

## ETIQUETTE SOS: AT THE BARBER

1. On your first appointment at a good salon or high-end barbershop, the barber should have a lengthy conversation with you about what you want. Embrace this. It's perfectly OK to bring in a picture or say you want a cut like, say, David Beckham (but, be realistic – they're barbers, not magicians).

2. Tell your barber what you do for a living. Work in a law firm? Tell him, and he's less likely to give you a skin fade by accident.

3. Let your barber know if you are the sort of person who will use products or whether you want something no-fuss – they can tailor a cut more specifically to how you live your life.

4. Be honest – they are going to see if you're thinning or greying so don't try to hide it. Work with them and get their advice on how best to address the issue.

5. Your barber should be good enough that they are as comfortable with scissors as clippers. If they reach for the clippers before the scissors, be a little wary.

6. At a traditional barbershop, where you wait your turn for whichever barber is free first, it's perfectly acceptable to wait for your preferred cutter (it's your hair, and if you don't want the guy in the butcher's apron waving the clippers around with reckless abandon near it, then that's fair enough).

**"I'll take him!"**

7. Don't feel you have to chat – but don't be a grumpy sod either.

8. Tip – 10% is about right. Feel free to offer that to the person who washes your hair if it's not the same person as the barber.

———

'WHY DON'T YOU GET A HAIRCUT?
YOU LOOK LIKE A CHRYSANTHEMUM.'

**P.G. WODEHOUSE**

———

## CUT A DASH: THREE ESSENTIAL HAIRCUTS

Your teens and early twenties are for experimenting with your hair – by your late twenties, you should know what looks good on you and stick with it – though a little honing and refining will go a long way. Haircuts are, despite appearances, a pretty simple business and there are, essentially, just three types: short, medium and long.

### *1. Short*

Ask for a classic short back and sides – layered through the top, possibly cut a touch shorter into the parting if you have one.

*Who's it for: This is the ultimate, go-to, standard look; it'll suit anyone big, small, curly, straight, thinning, greying, whatever.*

*Think: Steve McQueen (The Getaway), Montgomery Clift (A Place in the Sun)*

## 2. Medium

Almost a grown-out short back and sides. Ask for a graduated, side-parted cut, layered and with a little length to it. For more of a quiff – think young Elvis or Chet Baker – ask for a short, tight cut around the back and sides, left longer on top.

*Who's it for: This suits those with straighter hair better, and is extremely elegant when paired with a suit and tie.*

*Think: Alain Delon (The Sicilian Clan), Bryan Ferry (1976–78)*

## 3. Long

Let it grow, then ask a barber to keep it neat. Don't let it reach the shoulders and keep it clean and well maintained – a leave-in styling conditioner will give you a healthy, manageable barnet.

*Who's it for: Suits those with sharper, more angular faces and, when cared for properly, works as well with suit and tie as jeans and T-shirt. They key is keeping it fresh and groomed.*

*Think: Adam Driver (The Rise of Skywalker), Vincent Gallo (Buffalo '66)*

## STYLE IT OUT: GO GREY AND BALD GRACEFULLY

### *Silverfox: How to Go Grey*

Get yourself a bottle of hair dye, place
a towel over your shoulders, read the
instructions on the bottle carefully,
then put it back in the box and lob
it in the bin. For further confirmation
that dye is the devil's work ponder,
briefly, which looks better: George
Clooney or Rudy Giuliani as he
sweated out his hair dye shortly after
the 2020 US elections.

The reason hair dye looks unnatural is because it is. Instead,
embrace the elegance, wisdom and statesmanship silver hair
offers and any time your greyness bugs you, glance at a bald
man and count your blessings.

### *Thin on Top: How to Go Bald*

Ironically, the less hair you have, the more it needs cutting.
Keep thinning hair short, neat and at an even length all over.
Simply shaving it all off can work if you have a good head
shape, but is a bold move that may not suit everyone.

Baldness is not something to hide but to embrace. Not even
Bobby Charlton could pull off a combover and he had 100 caps
for England – so your chances of managing it in the monthly
client contact meeting are marginal.

·•————•·————•·

'ANYONE CAN BE CONFIDENT WITH
A FULL HEAD OF HAIR. BUT A
CONFIDENT BALD MAN – THERE'S
YOUR DIAMOND IN THE ROUGH.'

**LARRY DAVID**

·•————•·————•·

---

**FOUR OF A KIND**

**Nails:** Keep them short and clean.

**Eyebrows:** Ask your barber to keep them in nick. Tame them, don't overgroom or shape them, and avoid a monobrow by plucking the middle (but be careful or you can make yourself look startled).

**Nose:** Get a trimmer – they cost a tenner, for goodness sakes, and work really, really well – then use it if you ever want to go on a date again.

**Ears:** See nose, but more so.

# Skincare

## DAILY DUTY: CLEANSE AND MOISTURISE

Aside from waking you up in the morning and cleaning off the dirt of the day in the evening, a daily skincare routine will noticeably improve your appearance and keep wrinkles at bay.

### Step 1: Cleanse with a face wash

You wash the rest of yourself, so why forget about your face? Ideally, use morning and night but, if that's too much effort, then prioritise a nightly cleanse.

1.  Wash your hands (spreading germs and dirt onto your face defeats the object of it all).

2.  Dampen your face with lukewarm (not hot) water.

3.  Squeeze a ten-pence-sized squirt of face wash onto your palm.

4.  Lightly lather it between your palms and apply to your face in small circular motions for 30–60 seconds. Be gentle; don't scrub.

5.  Rinse off thoroughly and pat dry with a towel.

### Step 2: Moisturise

You should have two bottles of moisturiser on your bathroom shelf: a light one with an SPF for the daytime, and a richer, hydrating one for night.

1. Wash your face first, and make sure your skin is dry.

2. Squeeze a small amount of moisturiser into your palm, about the size of a penny.

3. Using small circular, massaging movements, start by applying to the middle of your face, around and on your nose, and then move onto your cheeks, forehead, neck and ears. Don't get too near your eyes.

4. If you have some stubble, go over that (but avoid anything too lengthy or your beard).

## FACETIME: SKINCARE EXTRAS

Nothing can turn back the clock, or magically undo the signs of a heavy night, but going the extra mile with your skincare may ward off premature ageing.

**Exfoliate:** Get gritty with an exfoliator – a face wash with tiny abrasive particles that removes dead skin cells and reduces the chance of ingrown hairs. Approach it as you would your usual face wash but take a little longer over it, and only use twice a week.

**Serum:** A bit like a super-charged, super-concentrated skin multivitamin, serum is a lightweight liquid that is easily absorbed and sinks in deeper than your moisturiser. Apply daily after cleansing and before moisturising – just a couple of drops will do the job.

**Eye cream:** If you have noticed crow's feet and fine lines around your eyes, then it's time to pat (not rub) a tiny amount of eye cream on daily – don't get too close to your actual eye or it can it play red-eye havoc for hours.

'THE SKIN UNDER YOUR EYES IS STARTING TO LOOK LIKE HUGH HEFNER'S BALL SACK.'

**JACOB, *CRAZY STUPID LOVE***

# Smelling Good

## ON THE SCENT: WHICH IS WHICH?

**Aftershave:** Designed to be put onto freshly shaved skin – the alcohol content disinfects any nicks and cuts, and speeds up healing – but only smells good for a few hours.

**Eau de cologne:** Longer-lasting than aftershave. 'Cologne' is also a catch-all term for men's fragrance.

**Eau de toilette:** This is most modern male 'perfumes' or fragrances. Stronger and longer-lasting than aftershave and eau de cologne.

**Eau de parfum:** The strongest on the market, but less usual for men's fragrance.

## FRAGRANCE FINESSE

Early memories of upping your fragrance game usually starts as a teenager, heading out wearing either a squirt of your dad's or a haze of Lynx, with a fake ID card safely tucked in your pocket and just one thing on your mind …

Things for you should have moved on since then, but choosing the right cologne and wearing it well can still be tricky – get it wrong and you permeate every corner of the office and cause headaches in the boardroom. A bad cologne can be just as unattractive as good cologne can be attractive.

**How to buy.** Try before you buy. Spray it onto your skin, not just a tester card, and leave for 20-30 minutes to develop. Avoid the duty-free temptation of trying too many at the same time or you won't be able to distinguish between them.

**How to apply.** Fragrance responds well to natural body heat, so apply a couple of squirts to the pulse points on your wrist and neck; if you're fresh from the shower, squirt your chest too. Remember, eau de toilette is more potent than a normal aftershave.

**Don't overdo it.** Remember that you will get used to your fragrance and, after a while, may not be able to smell it as much. More is not always better – smelling someone before (or after) you can see them is always a bit disconcerting.

**FYI** *Store fragrances in the cool (think bedroom not bathroom) and away from sunlight (so in its box). On average a bottle will last 3-5 years; heavier scents last longer than lighter, citrus ones.*

---

'GOOD MANNERS AND GOOD COLOGNE ARE WHAT TRANSFORMS A MAN INTO A GENTLEMAN'

**TOM FORD**

## IN THE KNOW: FRAGRANCE FAMILIES

**Chypre** (say 'sheep-ra'): Intense, warm and dry. Mediterranean-inspired with bergamot, citrus, oakmoss, leather and wood. Grown-up and complex.

**Fougère** (say 'foo-share'): Traditional and masculine. Light top notes (what you smell first) such as lavender, bergamot or citrus with woody or spicy undertones (tobacco, sandalwood, amber). The most likely to help you get lucky, according to numerous surveys.

**Oriental:** Strong, exotic and heavy. Musk, incense, spice, sandalwood, vanilla. With a tendency to linger, it is a bit much for the boardroom and best saved for the evening.

**Aquatic:** Light, fresh and clean. Citrus, marine, water, herbs. Think summertime, holidays and hot weather.

**Citrus:** Light and clean. Tangerine, grapefruit, bergamot. Best for daytime, perfect for holidays.

**Aromatic:** Herby and fresh. Lavender, rosemary, sage, grasses, along with citrus or spice. A bit of a vague catch-all group, and the basis for many fragrances.

# Treatments

The spa was once a female stronghold, and in days gone by a solo male might have raised an eyebrow or two. Luckily, things have changed, and many spas now offer a range of treatments for everyone, along with some gender-specific grooming options. Take your pick.

## MASSAGE KNOW-HOW

The up-close-and-personal side of spa treatments can be intimidating. Starting with a massage can be a good idea – you know what to expect, and you are guaranteed to feel pretty good afterwards.

**Scrub up.** Take off your watch; switch off your phone. It's social to have a shower beforehand. Arrive, clean and ready, 15 minutes or so before your appointment to sort out paperwork. This is not the time to screech up sweaty and flustered at the last minute.

**Drink up.** Avoid treatments if you have a bad hangover; it's likely to make you feel worse – and think of what you are putting the therapist through. Make sure you are hydrated (this goes for most treatments, not just massages), and stay hydrated afterwards.

**Communicate (or not).** Talk to your therapist about any aches or twinges and flag any problem areas or allergies. Idle barber's-chair style chat is not expected, so let them get on with their job – the clock is running, so don't waste your time on small talk.

**Be honest.** You may have asked for hard pressure (be honest, you probably will have), but drop the no-pain-no-gain attitude and pipe up if it is too much. The aim is to relax and loosen your muscles, not have you walking into the office the next day like Frankenstein's monster.

**Simple decency.** Wondering if you ditch your smalls? It's mostly what you are comfortable with: tighter underwear or (dry) swimming trunks are fine; big baggy boxers might get in the way. The towels are there to keep your modesty with surprising effectiveness (and your therapist really isn't interested anyway). And never, ever, make a dodgy joke, even if you (think you) are being ironic.

'MASSAGE IS THE ONLY FORM OF PHYSICAL PLEASURE TO WHICH NATURE FORGOT TO ATTACH CONSEQUENCES.'

**ROBERT BREAULT**

## ALTERNATIVE ACTION

If a massage is too much skin-on-skin for you, then a facial might be a better option. Still too close for comfort? Try a scalp massage – you are probably used to a stranger washing your hair at the barber's, so this isn't so different.

## BEAUTY TIPS

Treatments are a service, and they are personal, so a 10–20% tip is the order of the day. There's no need to be rummaging for notes in the pocket of your gown and handing over cash in the treatment room; you can either add it when you settle up or leave it in one of the little envelopes at the desk.

## SOCIAL DISTANCE

'Dude … stop the spread, please. It's a space issue' … just as the signs on the Metro told New Yorkers, the same goes for saunas, steam rooms and Jacuzzis – manspreading is below-the-belt behaviour, and equally as creepy is spreading alpha-male tentacle arms wide around the edge of the Jacuzzi. Keep yourself to yourself and don't even consider losing the trunks or towel – those kinds of freedoms will have you kicked out.

# Sleep

## KNOW YOUR ROBES

Dressing gowns are correctly made of silk, cotton or wool, and are intended to bridge the gentleman's style gap between waking and dressing. Bath robes are a more practical workhorse - made of towelling, to be flung on after the shower for a final dry of the skin. Even more correctly, men traditionally fasten their dressing gown left over right, and women right over left. Will you remember, or does it really matter? Probably not.

## AN ODE TO SLIPPERS

There is only one point to a pair of slippers and that is that they must be the most comfortable footwear in history. If they are, do not accept carping from other halves, friends, the postman, the kids or anyone else. If they have bits hanging off them, but are comfortable - then they are fine. If they are pink leopard print, with yellow tassels and polka dot inserts, but are comfortable - they are fine. If the dog has chewed them up, they leave a toxic vapour trail, but are comfortable - they are fine. Brook no arguments about this: a man's slippers are his best friend and nobody's opinion about them except the wearer's is valid.

## SEVEN STEPS TO A DECENT NIGHT'S SLEEP

Your sleep-wake cycle is dictated by your circadian rhythm – a natural body clock that rules your body, brain and hormones. But, just like any boss, you can manage up and work it to your advantage.

1.  *See the light.* Tricky in the winter months or if you work in a strip-lighted high-rise, but increasing your exposure to natural daylight will help you sleep.

2.  *No screens.* The blue light emitted from phone, tablet and laptop screens can trick your body into thinking it is daytime, so turn off your screens before you get into bed.

3. *Exercise*. Save your post-workout high for the daytime, not the evening. Mood-boosting hormones produced after exercise may keep you awake, even if you have tired yourself out.

4. *Cut coffee*. Caffeine can stay in the bloodstream for six to eight hours, so skip afternoon and late-night coffees.

5. *Banish booze*. While an extra glass of red may help you wind down and doze off, alcohol can affect your sleep pattern later in the night, making you restless in the small hours.

6. *Ambience*. Your bedroom should be a relaxing place to be: quiet, calm and not too hot. Make sure you have a decent lining on your curtains or blackout blinds to make it properly dark.

7. *Perform*. A heady post-coital mix of relaxing oxytocin and sleep-inducing prolactin usually ensures – not always to everyone's delight – that you will swiftly power down and drift off.

'THE LAST REFUGE OF THE INSOMNIAC IS A SENSE OF SUPERIORITY TO THE SLEEPING WORLD.'

**LEONARD COHEN**

## KIT-OFF COMFORT

It can be argued that being in your birthday suit at night is good for your health. Losing the heavy pyjamas means that while you sleep, your body (and your bits) cool down and your temperature is easily regulated. Plus there are no waistbands to dig in, pyjama trouser legs to get twisted or tops to ride up, making it more comfortable. Just be sure to change those sheets regularly.

# Informal

◆◆————————◆◆————————◆◆

JEANS • T-SHIRTS AND POLOS
JUMPERS • CASUAL COATS
CASUAL SHOES • KEEPING COOL
SUNGLASSES • SMART CASUAL
INFORMAL EVENTS
PRIVATE MEMBERS' CLUBS

'NEVER WEAR ANYTHING
THAT PANICS THE CAT.'

P.J. O'ROURKE

# Balancing Act

It's easy to look good in the office: a smarter shirt than the guy
at the next desk, a better tie than the boss and you're done.
Casual is harder, but it's easy enough to get right if you strike
a balance: trainers can soften a smart chino; a good shirt can
smarten up a pair of shorts; a cashmere, rather than cotton,
hoodie elevates the comfortable into the classy. Being off-duty
doesn't need to mean a drop in standards – sometimes you
have to dress up to dress down to win at the casual game.

# Jeans

~~~~~~~~~~~~~~~~~~~~~~~~~~~~~~~~~~~~~~~~~~~~

## THE MULTITASKER: JEANS

It's likely that your jeans are the most worn item in your wardrobe, so taking the time to find a perfect pair makes perfect sense – as does spending a bit more on them. Work it out on price per wear, and they are surprisingly economic.

Leave the skinny-fit to the teenagers, the loose-legged to the skateboarders and the belted high-rise to your grandad. For most body shapes, a slim fit is the order of the day and for comfort, look for something with a little stretch.

You want your jeans to be not too wide, not too skinny, not too tight on the knee, not too baggy around the thigh. They shouldn't sit too low, or too high (so mid-rise). They should have a slight taper, but not so narrow at the bottom that they don't sit well on your shoe.

~~~~~~~~~~~~~~~~~~~~~~~~~~~~~~~~~~~~~~~~~~~~

## COLOUR CODED: DENIM WASHES

~ *Dark wash:* Not quite navy, the smartest on the denim spectrum and, handily, pairs with nearly everything.

~ *Medium wash:* Think vintage Levi's 501 – the classic casual denim colour.

~ *Acid/stone wash:* Best left in the 1980s.

~ *Light wash:* Best worn by Wham!

~ *White:* Only an Italian can.

## FABRIC UNRAVELLED

**Raw denim:** The choice of denim purists. The fabric has not been softened or pre-washed, meaning the 'fade' or worn-in look will be created by you, as you wear them. This requires some commitment: you need to break them in and they can be uncomfortable to start with.

**Selvedge denim:** Look inside the bottom of the leg side seam and, if it is selvedge, the edging looks like a woven band. This means the denim won't unravel, and it creates a clean look, but makes the jeans more expensive.

**Combine the two:** If you have the bank balance and the patience to wear them in, jeans made from selvedge, raw denim are the best combination for workmanship, longevity and the chance to make a pair of jeans truly your own.

(FYI) *Wash denim inside out, on a cold cycle, and keep it to a minimum – experts claim your denim should only go in the machine a couple of times a year. Given a regular airing, you'll be surprised how long they can go without seeing detergent.*

# T-Shirts and Polos

## FITS TO A T: HOW TO CHOOSE A T-SHIRT

~ The end of the seam along the top of your shoulders should end right at the edge of your shoulder, so the sleeves of the T-shirt fall at a right angle downwards.

~ Sleeves should end around the middle of your bicep – this allows you to show some definition in your arm, guns or no guns.

~ Mid-fly is the perfect length. Any longer and you shorten your legs; any shorter and it looks like it's shrunk.

~ It should neither be glued to your pecs nor hanging like a sack. Aim for a little definition over the chest and a little give over the torso.

~ A classic round neck suits everyone. If you dare to bear with a V-neck, keep it relatively high – no one wants to see your chest-rug blowing in the breeze.

~ Stick to 100% cotton. Jokes on a T-shirt are never funny, and keep it brand- and logo-free unless, of course, the brand is paying you to do their advertising.

## T-SHIRTS FOR GROWN-UPS: POLO SHIRTS

The pairing of your polo can define your day. Dress it up with chinos or a blazer, and you are sorted for smart casual when a shirt is a touch OTT. Partner with jeans and you can dress down a notch but still have a collar – classic smart casual, or perfect for working-from-home video calls. Sling one on with your shorts and you add a touch of smart that beats a T-shirt.

Smart yet sporty, textured in piqué cotton or simple in smooth plain cotton, the key – as always – is in the fit. Slimmer cuts tick the style box, but avoid anything too tight. Large logos make you look like a plumber and anything too baggy like the guy at the DIY store.

# Jumpers

## AN ODE TO THE HOODIE

Hoodie snobs are just men who have never worn a hoodie before. Because try one on, even for a minute, and you will be a convert for life. The hoodie is a warm hug that you wear. It's a friend in a time of need. It's the comfort blanket that it's acceptable for a grown man to take to the pub. It should have a generous hood and be neither tight-fitting nor too baggy. Cotton hoodies should should live forever, gently fading and becoming your oldest friend. More luxury merino or cashmere hoodies offer a more stylish option for those who don't want to give in entirely but be warned: wear one once, and you'll never go back.

## KNITWEAR RULES

~   Only wear natural materials: merino, alpaca or cashmere in winter, decent cotton in the summer.

~   Fit matters: your friendly baggy pullover is fine for a Sunday night in, but that's about it.

~   V-necks work with shirts, round-necks with T-shirts (and some collared shirts); turtlenecks work more casually (or if you're a 1960s dope-smoking jazz musician).

~ Christmas jumpers are for throwing on bonfires.

~ Jumpers should have sleeves. If it's warm, take your jumper off. If it's cold, put one on. At no point is there a halfway temperature where you need your body warm and your arms cool to justify a sleeveless jumper.

---

**CLASSIC KNIT: THE ARAN JUMPER**

Taking its name from the Aran Islands of the west coast of Ireland (and sometimes known as a fisherman sweater), the Aran jumper has just the right amount of detail and chunk. Cosy yet stylish, it's a winter wardrobe winner – take inspiration from those who wore one well:

~ Elvis Presley, *Jailhouse Rock* (1957)

~ Steve McQueen, *The Thomas Crown Affair* (1968)

~ Ryan O'Neal, *Love Story* (1970)

~ Billy Crystal, *When Harry Met Sally* (1989)

~ Chris Evans, *Knives Out* (2019)

~ Adam Driver, *House of Gucci* (2021)

---

'ANYONE CAN GET DRESSED UP
AND GLAMOROUS, BUT IT IS HOW
PEOPLE DRESS IN THEIR DAYS OFF
THAT ARE THE MOST INTRIGUING.'

**ALEXANDER WANG**

## IN THE KNOW: HOW TO CARE FOR WOOL AND CASHMERE

~ Whether by hand or in the machine, use a wool-wash liquid and skip the fabric conditioner.

~ Wash jumpers inside out and treat carefully when wet or they will grow arms like Mr Tickle.

~ Wool should be air-dried flat, on a towel, away from strong heat such as radiators or direct sun.

~ Never tumble-dry unless you want your jumper to fit a ten-year-old rather than your torso.

**FYI** *Knitted items should be stored folded; woven items can be hung (use padded hangers). For longer storage, put away clean and, for your best cashmere, use moth repellent such as cedar blocks and consider bagging them up for extra protection.*

# Casual Coats

**Harrington.** Versatile, stylish, simple and timeless, the Harrington is hard to beat as a go-to casual spring and summer jacket that can also pull double duty for business casual. More structured and stylish than a bomber. Famous wearers include Steve McQueen, Frank Sinatra and James Dean and, frankly, if it's good enough for them …

**Parka.** For cold weather, few coats offer the practicality of a parka. Made famous by 1960s mods, then co-opted by Oasis's Gallagher brothers, it should be warm first and stylish second. Down-filled versions offer the most insulation and work well only in the coldest months, with lighter, waterproof options more versatile.

**Peacoat.** Double-breasted and generally made from dark blue or black wool, its broad shape was originally designed to allow sailors a full range of movement. It means it should be roomy enough to contain a chunky knit jumper, or even a suit. Should really be buttoned up at all times to avoid a flapping front, though modern single-breasted variations avoid that issue (though aren't technically peacoats).

**Puffer jacket.** Super warm, comfortable and practical, they are the ideal travelling companion given how small they can pack down. A winter staple.

**Wax jacket.** The ideal outdoor jacket – rugged, waterproof and weather-beaten. Avoid the mouldy huntin', shootin', fishin' jacket and go for a more contemporary cut, but always with an eye to the traditional so it does not date. Re-wax every few years and you'll have a friend for life.

---

### ON THE MAP

British racing teams had been wearing Barbour jackets for over 40 years, but when Steve McQueen wore the Barbour A7 Motorcycle Jacket to the 1964 International Six Day Trials in East Germany, the wax jacket moved from functional to cool. The 1980s saw yuppies, royalty and Sloanes wearing the traditional Barbour as we think of it today; by the mid-2000s Barbours were being worn by headline acts at Glastonbury and the humble wax jacket was, once again, redefined as cool and iconic.

# Casual Shoes

## STYLE IT OUT: TRAINERS

There are trainers for every outfit – whether sporty, casual, hot, cold, wet or dry – and it's next to impossible to have hard and fast rules as to the right pair for every occasion. But there are some things to bear in mind:

~   Classic sneakers will rarely be wrong – they're classic for a reason.

~   Your trainers should never be the first thing someone notices.

~   Running shoes are for running, gym shoes are for the gym – never for jeans or shorts.

(FYI) *Deck shoes or loafers are a smarter summer look – worn without socks (or with secret ones) for a touch of continental style.*

# Keeping Cool

## HOW TO WEAR SHORTS

Moderation is key. Too baggy, and you look like a late 1990s skater; too long, and it just looks like you're wearing badly fitting trousers; too short and, well, nobody's grateful for a surprise glimpse of the conkers. Usually, somewhere between mid-thigh and the top of the knees is about right. Keep them tailored but not tight – thighs should not bulge – and classic sandy, olive, blue or red will rarely be wrong. A turn-up looks smart and will get the length just right. Patterned shorts are great for summer months – the bolder the short, the plainer the T-shirt or shirt – but keep them on the right side of the quiet/loud divide. People should not mistake them for a colour-blindness test.

## ESSENTIAL UPGRADE: PROPER SWIMWEAR

**Do** choose trunks tailored like shorts – they will look good lounging around the pool, but just as good in the bar.

**Don't** go too long or it can shorten the legs (but very short trunks only suit those with a physique to show off).

**Do** consider a side stripe to help visually lengthen the legs and, for those on the wider side, slenderise the thighs.

**Don't** choose bold, branded logos – nobody needs to know where you bought your trunks from. And never wear briefs – nobody needs to see that on their holiday.

## SUMMER FEET

**Sandals:** A smart choice. Brown leather tends to work best – but the darker the material, the more pasty the feet can look for those with pale skin. Keep them simple, without too many straps or buckles.

**Flip-flops:** The simpler, the better. Keep them slender, with a single V-shaped band for the toes (and leave the sliders for the gym). Flip-flops are for the day – once the sun is down, they are just that bit too casual. Remember that across the pond, flip-flops are called 'thongs'; men wearing thongs in Britain has a more uncomfortable meaning.

# Sunglasses

'WITH MY SUNGLASSES ON,
I'M JACK NICHOLSON. WITHOUT
THEM, I'M FAT AND 60.'

**JACK NICHOLSON**

## HOW TO SELECT SUNGLASSES

### Shape Assessment

**Work out your face shape, and then the general rule is to pick a pair that are the opposite …**

~ *Round:* A rectangular frame adds definition, but round frames can emphasise soft lines.

~ *Oval:* Most styles will suit, but try square or rectangular for contrast and definition.

~ *Triangular:* Generally, it's best to avoid aviators. Go for square or round frames; longer faces can be balanced with a wider frame.

~ *Square:* Soften with round, aviator-style frames.

## ON FILM: ICONIC EYEWEAR

Steve McQueen: 0714 Persols, *The Thomas Crown Affair* (1968)

Clint Eastwood: Ray-Ban Baloramas, *Dirty Harry* (1971)

Robert De Niro: Ray-Ban Caravans, *Taxi Driver* (1976)

Tom Cruise: Ray-Ban Wayfarers, *Risky Business* (1983)

Al Pacino: Linda Farrow 6031 Aviators, *Scarface* (1983)

Eddie Murphy: Porsche Design Carreras, *Beverly Hills Cop* (1984)

Will Smith: Ray-Ban 2030 Predators, *Men in Black* (1997)

Brad Pitt: Oliver Peoples 523, *Fight Club* (1999)

Ryan Gosling: Selima Optique Money 2 Aviators, *Drive* (2011)

Daniel Craig: Tom Ford Snowdons, *Spectre* (2015)

## LENS LESSONS

Lenses must have UV protection. Choose polarised for greater clarity in bright places, mirrored for those with light sensitivity or tinted to help in certain lights. Photochromic lenses react to light and automatically tint when you go from dark to light – they just look weird, so avoid.

## FIT FACTORS

Fit is important – they should fit snugly without pinching – you should not be pushing them up or down your nose constantly. Don't just put them on and admire how cool you look; move about a bit and check they stay put.

'MEN WANT THE SAME THING FROM THEIR UNDERWEAR THAT THEY WANT FROM WOMEN: A LITTLE BIT OF SUPPORT, AND A LITTLE BIT OF FREEDOM.'

**JERRY SEINFELD**

## FOUR OF A KIND

**Socks:** They matter more than you realise. White socks are for sport, novelty socks for children. Socks can add a clever pop of colour; more conservatively stick to classic blue, black or a tasteful grown-up stripe.

**Belts:** A smooth black or brown leather and a classic buckle. No mock croc or plate buckles – you're not on a Harley Davidson.

**Handkerchiefs:** A germ-spreading, pre-pandemic cloth of the past. Use a tissue.

**Underwear:** They should be in good nick and novelty-free. And VPL can affect guys too if your smalls are too tight or too baggy.

# Smart Casual

Let the details be your guide. Where are you going? Who are you going with? Who's hosting? What kind of event is it? What is the venue? It's better to be overdressed than underdressed – short of turning up in a dinner jacket to a BBQ, no one ever comments when someone looks smart, but many a judgement has been made when it's all too causal.

**FYI** *If it's an annual event, search hashtags on social media to see what kind of thing (sensible) people have worn before.*

## THE THREE DEGREES OF SMART CASUAL

### 1. Smart-smart casual

Think of it as a step-down from a suit. Chinos (or similar), an open-necked shirt and a blazer. If it's chilly, layer with a thin knit under your jacket. Wear proper shoes – Derbys, boots, loafers, etc. - not trainers.

*No denim, no T-shirts, no polo shirts, no sportswear.*

## 2. Smart casual

It's a matter of balance – if you loosen up in one area, you need to smarten up in another. Go for chinos or your best dark wash denim. A shirt is safest, or possibly a polo shirt. No need for a jacket if you have a collar; a merino zip-neck will keep you smart but cosy. You might get away with a plain, pressed, well-fitting T-shirt if everything else is looking sharp and you stick it on with a jacket.

*No sportswear, sometimes no T-shirts.*

### 3. Casual-smart casual

You need to look like you've made a bit of an effort. Decent denim; shirt, polo or T-shirt. Good-looking knits, not a sweatshirt or hoodie. Clean and plain-ish trainers.

*No sportswear.*

———•——•——•———

'IF YOU EVER SEE ME IN A SOCIAL
SETTING IN ANY SORT OF SPORTSWEAR,
THEN YOU KNOW I'M IN CRISIS.'

**BILL NIGHY**

———•——•——•———

# Informal Events

'Dinner party' may sound vintage – vol-au-vents, prawn cocktail, cheese fondue, coq au vin, black forest gateau, sherry trifle – but the dinner party is alive and well, and being asked for 'dinner' is different to being asked for 'supper'.

**Read the signs.** Take your cues from the hosts. Are they friends-with-influence, in-the-club types? A power couple or parvenus? Literary city types or townies in the country? Your boss, a client, an acquaintance or your friend? Then consider where you are going: Notting Hill flat, Chelsea townhouse or Hackney warehouse apartment? A just-left-London family home on the south coast, shiny new barn conversion or tumbling rural pile?

**Stay cool.** A dinner party is likely to be a smarter affair, with (what your host perceives to be) a eclectic mix of guests, flashier food and superior booze. They may even hire someone for the evening to take the coats and clear the plates. If the prospect of such social frisson and ceremony stirs up giddying levels of excitement, try to take it in your stride. Aim for polite nonchalance backed up by superb social skills – overenthusiasm is for children's parties, not a grown-up dinner party.

**Sit back and relax ...** On the other side of the coin, a 'kitchen supper' translates as a relaxed Friday evening with close friends and good food. This is the time to sit back and settle in with people you know well. It's all about eating something decent, well executed and a touch comforting – curry, sharing plates, slow-cooked meat, pasta – washed down with a glass or three too many in the cosiness of the kitchen. For most of us, this is the kind of social dining we really enjoy. The kitchen supper may not have entirely killed the dinner party, but it's given it a good run for its money.

## ETIQUETTE SOS: THE DINNER PARTY GUEST

**Rule 1:** Up your casual game, just a little. Your aim is to look as smart, or a touch smarter, than your hosts. Swap the T-shirt for a collar, and the everyday jeans for a pair of dark wash ones or chinos. For flashier hosts, wear a jacket (you can always take it off). Add some flair with touches of colour and pattern – it is the evening, not the office.

**Rule 2:** Be fashionably late. You know the drill: if they ask you over for 7.30pm, it really means 7.40pm, but no later than 7.45pm. Being early = social suicide.

**Rule 3:** Don't go empty-handed. A chilled bottle of fizz, wine, chocolates or flowers. Don't regift the bottle of plonk from the back of the cupboard.

**Rule 4:** Beg to Differ. There's no need to be boring, but strong differences of opinion can quickly turn from exuberant into argument. It's dinner, not Speaker's Corner, so know when to step off your box and shut up. If others are getting embarrassingly hot under the collar, come to the rescue with some clever humour and a swift change of topic.

**Rule 5:** Helping hand. For casual evenings, clear plates from the table, but don't stack the dishwasher; bring through serving plates, but don't wash the pans. For more formal dinners, guests are expected to stay front-of-house and not wander into the kitchen. Keep the water flowing, but never pour the wine in someone else's castle.

**Rule 6:** Last orders. The other guests have left and your host is dropping hefty hints about their early start, but you're holding out for another bottle of Merlot. Recognise when to check the Uber ETA – it's gone too far when your host is ordering for you and turning out the lights.

**Rule 7:** Say thank you. Text, email, letter, card – the choice is yours. For hosts with the most, send flowers the day before with a note saying how much you are looking forward to dinner; then feel suitably smug about your impeccable social graces when they are in pride of place at the main event.

## LIFE SKILL: PRE-DINNER DRINKS

At the smarter end of the dinner party spectrum, drinks in the drawing room precede dinner in the dining room.

~ When you are asked what you would like to drink, scan what others are drinking and, if your host is hovering with a bottle of fizz and a clean glass in hand, don't ask for a G&T.

~ Hit the 'hellos' with your glass in your left hand – it frees up your right for shaking hands.

~ Try to eat canapés in one mouthful. If there is dipping sauce, remember health and safety by only dipping once, *before* you've bitten into it.

~ If you happen to know who you are sitting next to at dinner, don't talk to them at the drinks. Talk to other people pre-meal and you have an intact arsenal of conversation when you take your seat.

**FYI** *A drawing room is a smart, elegant living room – without the TV and family clutter. You can only have a drawing room if you have a second less formal sitting room, and even then you can only really claim one if your house is more* Downton Abbey *than semi-detached.*

## PERSONALITY PLAY: SEATING PLANS

In Britain, couples generally don't sit next to each other at the table, whether it is a dinner party or a wedding reception. They spend enough time together, so talking to someone else usually adds a little spice to the evening, and it provides plenty of fresh chat for the car on the way home.

Mix old friends with new and quiet guests with good conversationalists. The socially confident can kick-start the shy, and the extroverts lure the introverts. Keep it slick and don't make a fuss – as the late Duke of Edinburgh hangrily once said, 'Bugger the table plan, give me my dinner!'.

'IN CALIFORNIA, OF COURSE, THEY NEVER BREAK UP COUPLES AT DINNER FOR FEAR OF WHAT MIGHT HAPPEN IF SOMEONE'S HUSBAND WERE SEATED NEXT TO SOMEONE ELSE'S VERY YOUNG GIRLFRIEND. BUT DINNERS WITH COUPLES SEATED NEXT TO ONE ANOTHER ARE ALWAYS DEADLY DULL, WHICH IS WHY THERE ARE ALMOST NO GOOD DINNER PARTIES IN THE ENTIRE STATE OF CALIFORNIA.'

**NORA EPHRON**

## DECENT DONATIONS

Very busy friends or hosts of larger gatherings may ask you
to bring something along, for example cheese or pudding.
Desperate offerings from the Tesco Express en route – arctic
roll, Vienetta, shrink-wrapped Brie, Baby Bell, Boursin – can't
even be passed for ironic. Do better and get to the deli in time.

## DINNER PARTY FAUX PAS

~  Instagramming the food (#tablescape).

~  Going on about your children.

~  Lecturing on cooking process.

~  Outrageously flirting with someone else's partner.

~  Getting slur-and-stumble plastered.

~  Preaching about house prices.

~  Pontificating about politics.

~  Bluffing (badly) about the wine.

~  Angling for a business introduction.

~  Talking business.

'IT IS VERY VULGAR TO TALK ABOUT
ONE'S BUSINESS. ONLY PEOPLE LIKE
STOCKBROKERS DO THAT, AND THEN
MERELY AT DINNER PARTIES.'

**ALGERNON,** *THE IMPORTANCE OF BEING EARNEST*

# Private Members' Clubs

The wood-panelled, cigar-smoky, leather-chaired gentlemen's clubs of St James may still be ticking along (most even letting women in nowadays), but clubland has certainly moved on. The billiard rooms have been replaced with gyms, the libraries with co-working spaces. Private members' clubs each have a distinct personality and breed of member: stage and screen, traditionalists and aristos, media and arts, influencer and A-lister, the list goes on. Whatever the niche, they come with a united mission: to provide a sanctum for like-minded people with excellent service, facilities and privacy. A home from home, if you like. Respecting the house rules, therefore, is a must.

~ Always check the dress code – every club has one in varying degrees of smartness and complexity, and even timings on what you can wear where and when. The most traditional insist on a jacket and tie, many specify no denim, most no sportswear and some no T-shirts. A baseball cap or fleece will see most doors shut on you. Do your research.

~ Never go wandering without checking-in. Make yourself known to reception on arrival; if you are a guest, your host should have told them to expect you.

~ Coats, hats, luggage and umbrellas should be left at the cloakroom – most clubs insist on this.

~ Switch your phone on silent; this is the place for text messages only.

~ The focus is on pleasure, so laptops, paperwork and office-type paraphernalia are banned except in designated business-friendly areas.

~ Be cool. It's likely you will see familiar faces from the great and good. Don't stare; never ask for a selfie.

~ Photography is mostly banned, as is posting snaps on social media, and this is rigorously enforced. Don't get you or your host ousted for the sake of a few likes.

~ Never ask someone to recommend you for membership – this is something that must be offered, never requested. Asking to hang on their coat-tails can be embarrassing for everyone.

'THE WEARING OF STRING VESTS IS FULLY UNACCEPTABLE AND WHOLLY PROSCRIBED BY CLUB RULES. THERE IS ENOUGH DISTRESS IN THE WORLD ALREADY.'

**GROUCHO CLUB BOOK OF RULES**

# Polished

◆◆────────◆◆────────◆◆

**CONFIDENCE AND CHARISMA • DRINK
WINE • FOODIE • CULTURE VULTURE
MUSIC • WATCHES • BOOKS • DRIVING**

'EXPERIENCE TELLS
YOU WHAT TO DO;
CONFIDENCE ALLOWS
YOU TO DO IT.'

**STAN SMITH**

# Confidence and Charisma

Charm. Magnetism. Presence. The guy who isn't the best looking or the sharpest dressed (although that helps) but walks in and manages to turn heads, seal deals and instantly connects. We assume that he was born with 'it' as, after all, we tend to pigeonhole our own levels of confidence to assume we simply aren't that guy.

The good news is that the tricks of his trade can be learnt. As humans, we need to feel appreciated, respected and like we belong. That guy makes other people feel all of those things but, above all, he makes them feel important. Here's how he does it …

**Total recall:** Remember them, but not just their name. Remember something they have told you. Recollect where they went on holiday, their wife's name, that they have kids or the team they support.

**Centre of attention:** Give them your undivided attention. Decent eye contact (but not staring), positive body language (body and feet facing them) and no phone checking (even if it rings or pings).

**Listen up:** Being heard makes us feel worthwhile, so tune in. Ask relevant questions, link back to what has been said earlier in the conversation – prove you are really listening to them.

**All seeing eye:** Comment on the big stuff. A promotion, an engagement, a house move (but be 100% sure about that pregnancy bump). With lesser friends or colleagues, don't mention things you've learnt about via social media or you may seem unnervingly stalker-like.

**School of thought:** It's flattering when your opinion and ideas matter, so ask their advice. Whether it's trivial (a restaurant recommendation) or more serious (a business decision), make them feel like a valued 'expert'.

**Inside story:** From playground to professional, there is little more thrilling than being in on a 'secret'. No need to spread mindless gossip or break an NDA clause, but confiding in someone creates immediate rapport. It need only be a little titbit – it's all in the drama of the delivery.

**Mind share:** Make personal recommendations. It may be restaurants or hotels; a lesser-known holiday destination; an interesting how-to. You can be pretty sure that they will look into it for themselves and share it with someone else – making you the in-the-know expert.

**Gift of time:** We are all busy. Even when we are less busy, we still say we are busy. Time is precious, so acknowledge it. Whether it's a business meeting, an out-of-the-office coffee, a quick drink after work or even a pint with a mate, always let them know that you've appreciated their time.

**Crack them up:** Humour, sarcasm, swearing, shocking or being risqué is all about timing, and making other people laugh (for the right reasons) is always a winner. And laughing at other people's jokes makes them feel like they are winning too.

---

### GET INVOLVED: SOFTEN

A handy acronym on how to look like you have a clue. Use when face to face to feign interest, use in meetings to seem engaged, or to elevate the delivery of your monthly presentations. Newsreaders are SOFTEN pros, so watch and learn:

**S**mile – be friendly and welcoming.

**O**pen body language – no crossed arms, fiddling or timid gestures.

**F**orward and facing – face them and lean forward, just a little.

**T**ouch – don't go OTT, so shaking hands for business / a brief man-hug for pleasure.

**E**ye contact – connect, don't stare.

**N**od – acknowledge and affirm what they say with a light nod.

FYI *Done well, this one's particularly effective.*

'PEOPLE WILL FORGET WHAT YOU SAID.
THEY WILL FORGET WHAT YOU DID.
BUT THEY WILL NEVER FORGET
HOW YOU MADE THEM FEEL.'

**MAYA ANGELOU**

## 1-2-3 MONEY! SEVEN STEPS TO SELFIE SUCCESS

1. *Lighting:* Avoid warts-and-all bright lighting or a startling camera flash.

2. *Feet:* Facing the camera.

3. *Shoulders:* Pull slightly back, position at a slight angle.

4. *Head:* 10–15 degrees away from the camera, slightly tilted.

5. *Chin:* Slightly down (avoid a double, but tilt too high and you risk seeing up your nostrils).

6. *Eyes:* Stare at the lens.

7. *Smile:* Try saying 'money' not 'cheese'. Works every time.

'A SELFIE A DAY
KEEPS THE FRIENDS AWAY.'

**ANON**

# Drink

## LIFE SKILL: ESSENTIAL DRINKS

*Triple whammy: the three drinks every man should be able to make, and make very well ...*

### The Perfect G&T

*Proportions:* Mix one part gin with three parts tonic water.

Fill a collins, copa or highball glass to the top with ice. For a double, pour over 50ml gin and top up with approximately 150ml tonic. Add a slice of lime.

**FYI** *Don't let the side down with cheap tonic water. Use a slice of lemon for a more delicate flavour; don't squeeze any citrus into the gin as it masks the aromas of the botanicals.*

### Bloody Mary

*Proportions:* Mix one part vodka with two parts tomato juice.

Fill a highball glass to the top with ice. Pour over 50ml vodka, and 250ml tomato juice. Add a squeeze of lemon, a few shakes of Worcestershire sauce and a couple dashes of Tabasco. Finish with a pinch of black pepper and celery salt and stir. Finish by adding a short celery stick to the glass.

**FYI** *Smoked Tabasco adds an interesting twist; add grated horseradish or mustard powder for an extra kick. Swap the vodka for tequila for a Bloody Maria, substitute with gin for a Red Snapper, use absinthe for a Bloody Fairy ... or garnish with a sausage for a Slutty Mary (please don't).*

## Pimm's

*Proportions:* Mix one part Pimm's No.1 with three parts lemonade.

Pimm's is easiest made in a jug; use plenty of ice and stir well. Add some fresh mint leaves, a few slices of cucumber and, if you must, some strawberries (but stop there – leave the fruit salad for pudding).

**FYI** *For a more sophisticated taste, replace the lemonade in part or fully with tonic water.*

·———··———··

'WE DRINK BECAUSE IT'S GOOD, BECAUSE IT FEELS BETTER THAN UNBUTTONING YOUR COLLAR, BECAUSE WE DESERVE IT. WE DRINK BECAUSE IT'S WHAT MEN DO.'

**ROGER STERLING,** *MAD MEN*

·———··———··

## EYE FOR DETAIL: SIX MIXOLOGY RULES

1.  Ice is essential. Pack glasses with plenty.

2.  Use the right glass (highball, tumbler, stemmed cocktail, etc.) and chill before using.

3.  Forget about flavoured gins or supermarket substitutes – choose classic, established brands.

4.  Don't forego the extras – egg whites, bitters, olives, orange twist, lime wedge, etc. If they are in a classic recipe, they play an important part.

5.  Shake well and shake hard. Use a shaker that is big enough to allow the ingredients to mix well.

6.  Drink up. Harry Craddock said that cocktails should be drunk quickly, 'while it's laughing at you'. No hanging around then.

'INTOXICATED? THE WORD DID NOT EXPRESS IT BY A MILE. HE WAS OILED, BOILED, FRIED, PLASTERED, WHIFFLED, SOZZLED, AND BLOTTO.'

**P.G. WODEHOUSE, *JEEVES AND WOOSTER***

## ICONS: MIXOLOGIST AND BARMAN – HARRY CRADDOCK (1875-1963)

Fancy winding down on Friday night with Satan's Whiskers or a Fallen Angel? *The Savoy Cocktail Book* by Harry Craddock was published in 1930 and is a bible of 750 of his cocktail recipes. Craddock's most famous cocktail was the White Lady, but he was prolific in his creations. Famous examples include the Rattlesnake, Stomach Reviver, Thunderclap, Between-the-Sheets, Parisian Blonde, Income Tax, Hanky Panky, Gloom-Chaser and the famous Corpse Reviver 'to be taken before 11 o'clock or whenever steam and energy are needed'.

Craddock spent many years working in America and claimed to have made the last cocktail in America before Prohibition set in. He returned to the UK and made his name at The Savoy's American Bar, mixing cocktails for celebrities, politicians and influencers of the day. His waxwork was even in Madame Tussauds.

No one understood the allure of a hotel bar quite like Craddock, and he left his own mark, figuratively and literally. In 1927 he buried a cocktail shaker filled with White Lady in the wall of The Savoy's American Bar, which has never been found.

## DRINK LIKE THE STARS: FIVE ICONIC COCKTAILS

### 1. Drink like ... Don Draper: Old Fashioned

*Glass: Rocks or old fashioned*

*Technique: Stirred, never shaken*

- ~ 50ml bourbon or rye whiskey
- ~ ½ teaspoon sugar
- ~ 3 dashes Angostura Bitters
- ~ 1 tsp water
- ~ Orange peel

*Method:* Combine the bitters and sugar in the glass, add the water to help it dissolve. Add ice cubes, pour over the whiskey and gently stir. Express the orange peel over the glass (meaning twist it between your thumb and forefinger to release aroma and oil), then drop in.

### 2. Drink like ... Jack Kerouac: Margarita

*Glass: Cocktail*

*Technique: Shaken, not stirred*

- ~ 50ml blanco or reposado tequila
- ~ 25ml fresh lime juice
- ~ 25ml triple sec (e.g. Cointreau)
- ~ Salt
- ~ Lime wedges

*Method:* Rub the rim of the glass with lime and roll in the salt to form a light crust. Fill a shaker with ice cubes, add the tequila, lime juice and triple sec, then shake. Fill the glass with (new) ice, strain over the contents and serve with a lime wedge.

───◆──◆──◆───

'SHE'S FROM MEXICO, SEÑORES, AND SHE'S LOVELY TO LOOK AT, EXCITING AND PROVOCATIVE.'

*ESQUIRE MAGAZINE* (1953), FIRST DESCRIBING A MARGARITA

───◆──◆──◆───

### 3. Drink like ... Ernest Hemmingway: Daiquiri

*Glass: Coupe or cocktail*

*Technique: Shaken, not stirred*

~   50ml light rum (e.g. Bacardi)
~   25ml lime juice
~   10ml sugar syrup

*Method:* Fill a shaker with ice cubes; add the rum, lime juice and sugar syrup. Shake, then strain into the glass.

## 4. Drink like ... James Bond: Vesper Martini

*Glass: Martini*

*Technique: Shaken not stirred*

- ~ 60ml London dry gin
- ~ 20ml vodka
- ~ 10ml Lillet Blanc / white vermouth
- ~ Lemon peel

*Method:* As Bond instructed in *Casino Royale*: 'Three measures of Gordon's, one of vodka, half a measure of Kina Lillet [vermouth]. Shake it very well until it's ice-cold, then add a large thin slice of lemon peel.'

## 5. Drink like ... Stanley Tucci: Negroni

*Glass: Coupe*

*Technique: Shaken not stirred*

- ~ 50ml gin
- ~ 25ml sweet vermouth
- ~ 25ml Campari
- ~ Orange slice

*Method:* Fill a shaker with ice cubes, add the gin, vermouth and Campari, shake and then strain into the glass. Lightly squeeze in a few drops from the orange slice before dropping in.

## AFTER DINNER KNOW-HOW:
## THE FINEST DIGESTIFS

*Generous measures compulsory. Company recommended.*
*Cigar optional.*

**Rum:** Try a dark rum; look for something with a bit of age on it.

(FYI) *Drink neat, or on the rocks. Overproof rums may also need a dash of water.*

**Brandy:** A Cognac XO (Extra Old) is the oldest – even better choose one from a single estate.

(FYI) *Hold a brandy balloon with the round of the glass resting in your palm, and the stem between your first two fingers – the heat from your hand will open up the aromas.*

**Whisky:** Skip the Scotch for a single malt; the distinguished gent knows his favourite (Speyside, Lowlands, Highlands, Islay, Campbeltown and Islands).

(FYI) *Adding a dash of water is fine, adding ice is not.*

# Wine

## IN THE KNOW: SERVING WINE

**Size matters.** Red wine glasses are larger than white wine glasses to allow the 'bouquet' (smell/aroma) to give off its best. Whites don't have the same aromatic qualities and are drunk chilled, so are served in a smaller glass. Know which is which before you offer to pour.

**Don't overfill.** It's not a sign of generosity; it makes you look like you don't know what you are doing. Pour no more than a third of the glass for reds and just under half for whites – usually just shy of the widest point of the glass.

**Be cool.** White wines should be chilled. Serve plonk from the supermarket as cold as possible and keep it on ice, but a decent white only needs about 20 minutes in the fridge. Serve it too cold and you kill the joy and complexity of a good wine.

**Hold it.** White wine glasses (or anything chilled in a stemmed glass; so champagne, Martini, cocktails, etc.) should be held by the stem. Red wine glasses can be held by either the stem or the bowl – holding it by the stem looks more cultivated.

## WINE: BLUFFER'S TALK

*Don't be a bore, don't be a fool ...*

**Don't say:** 'This is a nice drop. Is it very old?'
**Do say:** 'Beautifully balanced, with an elegant finish.'

**Don't say:** 'Doesn't taste of much.'
**Do say:** 'Not much nose – possibly a little young, or needs to open up.'

**Don't say:** 'Smells a bit funny.'
**Do say:** 'It's corked.'

**Don't say:** 'That bottle's a bit old and dusty.'
**Do say:** 'This has a nice bit of age on it.'

**Don't say:** 'Red from Bordeaux.'
**Do say:** 'Claret'

'I'M AFRAID MOST OF THE PEOPLE
WE GET IN HERE DON'T KNOW
A BORDEAUX FROM A CLARET.'

**BASIL FAWLTY,** *FAWLTY TOWERS*

## ETIQUETTE SOS: ORDERING AND TASTING

Ordering and tasting wine can be as intimidating as being picked on in an algebra lesson, particularly if you are in esteemed company. Whether you are impressing on a first date or simply surviving when your boss puts you on the spot, here are some top tips to order and taste by …

### How to Order

~ *Relax.* Take the wine list and leisurely peruse. Don't rush or look panicked.

~ *Scan.* Earmark a few bottles that fall within your price range and that you recognise (claret, New Zealand Sauvignon Blanc, Chianti, etc.).

~ *Canvass.* Ask, casually, what everyone is thinking of ordering and that will lead you to red, white or both.

~ *Ask.* The sommelier is there to help. Point to something on the list in your price range so that they can make budget-friendly suggestions – they are used to being discreet.

## *How to Taste*

~ *Check.* When the wine arrives at the table, be sure it is what you ordered (check the vintage too).

~ *Swirl.* Once a little is poured in your glass, give it a moment to 'breathe'. Keep the bottom of the glass on the table and swirl it gently.

~ *Smell.* Give it a quick sniff; this is to check whether it is corked (see below).

~ *Sip.* This isn't to check whether you like it, it's to double-check that it is up to scratch.

~ *Acknowledge.* A nod and a polite, 'That's fine, thank you' will do.

**FYI** *It is widely estimated that 1–3% of bottles with corks are 'corked' or tainted. Corked wine isn't bad for you – it's just not nice to drink. It smells unpleasantly musty, a bit like when a wet dishcloth gets stinky. Screwcaps dramatically reduce the risk of a wine becoming corked to near zero, so tasting these is more of a ritual than a necessity. Just go with it.*

### EYE FOR DETAIL: CHAMPAGNE

**The real deal:** Champagne can only be called 'champagne' when it is from the Champagne region of France, is made from Pinot Nior, Pinot Meunier and Chardonnay grapes, and is fizzed through a secondary fermentation in the bottle known as *méthode champenoise*.

**Vintage vs non-vintage:** Look at the label: a vintage bottle of champagne features a year whereas a non-vintage has no date. That doesn't mean non-vintage is no good – it is a highly skilled blend of grapes from different years, and top champagne houses won't put their name to anything substandard.

**Glasses:** It's easy to feel a bit like Jay Gatsby when sipping from a champagne coupe (saucer), but it may be doing more for your ego than the champagne. Supposedly modelled on the shape of a woman's breast – the jury's out on whether it was inspired by Marie Antoinette's or Helen of Troy's – your bubbly can go very flat, very quickly in such a wide glass. Taller, thinner flutes keep things fizzy.

**Substitutions:** French fizz produced outside of Champagne is called *crémant* and the Spanish equivalent is *cava* – both undergo the secondary in-bottle fermentation and a decent bottle of either of these can see off cheap champagne. Prosecco outsells champagne across the globe, but its secondary fermentation happens in a tank not a bottle, meaning a simpler flavour which can err on the sweeter side (cue grotty hangover).

# Foodie

**Asparagus:** Yes, you do eat it with your fingers when it's served on it's own, for example as a starter.

**Bread roll:** Break the bread into individual bite-sized pieces with your hands (never cut with a knife) and spread on a little butter using your butter knife. Eat and repeat.

**Cheese:** Never cut the 'nose' off a triangular cheese – cut a sliver from the long side. Cut a triangle out of a round cheese (like a slice of pizza). For a square or rectangular piece such as Cheddar, slice off the side.

'MARGE, YOU KNOW IT'S RUDE
TO TALK WHEN MY MOUTH IS FULL.'

**HOMER SIMPSON**

**Dietary requirements:** Allergic to dairy? Break out in hives near mustard? Tell your host in advance as it is inconvenient (actually, rude) to pipe up on arrival. Be sure it is for your health, not your keto diet.

**Enthusiasm:** Always compliment the chef.

**Fingerbowls:** Briefly dip your fingers in, then dry them on your napkin. And we all know the one about Queen Victoria drinking hers …

**Getting down:** Desperate for the gents? Try to hold on, preferably until after the main course (or at least never leave the table mid-course). Refrain from slipping outside and lighting up until after the meal.

**Helping yourself:** Offer side dishes, sauces and water before digging in. Finish what is on your plate before reaching for seconds.

**Isolate:** Keep phones on silent and put them away. Expecting an important call? Tell people in advance. Need to check your email? Nip to the gents.

**Jargon:** The menu may say '*Lapin à la moutarde*', but you only need to say, 'I'll have the rabbit' or you'll sound overly pretentious.

**KLP (knife-like-pen):** Knives are for cutting up food, not to be held with affection. Hold the handle firmly in your palm and with your index finger resting on the top of the handle.

**Limits:** Go in for seconds, but devouring thirds will make people think you can't feed yourself.

**Mussels:** Use an empty mussel shell as a pair of tweezers to ease out the mollusc with surprising effectiveness.

**Napkins:** Leave on your chair if you get down during the meal; leave unfolded to the left of your place setting at the end. And don't call them serviettes.

**Oysters:** Spear or slurp? The choice is yours. Either use the little oyster fork to lift it from the shell, or just use the fork to loosen it (even if shucked) before bringing the shell to your lips and tipping. Chew or swallow whole? Again, the choice is yours.

**Peas:** Squash onto the top of your fork, squish into your mash. You aren't five years old, so don't turn over your fork.

**Quaff:** Know your limits. Don't be the boring boozehound embarrassing the table.

**Resting position:** Rest your cutlery, mid-meal, in a twenty-past-eight position with the tines of the fork facing downwards.

When you are finished, place the knife and fork (with tines facing up) in a six-thirty position, with the handles facing your tummy.

**Soup:** Scoop away from you and tip the liquid into your mouth from the nearside edge. Only tilt your bowl (away from you) for the last couple of mouthfuls; only mop up with your bread when eating off a tray in front of *EastEnders*.

**Timing:** Start when the whole table has been served; the end goal is a loosely synchronised finish with the rest of the table.

**Unaccustomed:** Inexperienced with escargots? Fearful of fish on the bone? If you find yourself clueless, just hang back. Watch and learn from the most cultured companion at the table.

**Vulgar:** No chewing with your mouth open, no talking with your mouth full, no slurping or burping. Blame any windy surprises on the dog.

**Waste:** Eat up. In Britain it is polite to finish everything.

**X-factor:** If you are cooking for other people, stick to tried and tested. Your guests don't want you stuck in the kitchen sweating over a soufflé.

**Yuck:** Don't like what you have been served? See 'Waste'.

**Zone:** Keep elbows in and, even if you are built on the large side, sit up straight and don't loll in your chair.

'ONE OF MY MOST FAVOURITIST MEALS
IS DUCK À L'ORANGE, BUT I DON'T KNOW
HOW TO SAY THAT IN FRENCH.'

**DEL BOY, *ONLY FOOLS AND HORSES***

## HOME COOK: NINE RESTAURANT-INSPIRED COOKBOOKS

~ For (better) pub grub: *The Hand and Flowers Cookbook* – Tom Kerridge

~ For comfort: *Dishoom: From Bombay with Love* – Shamil Thakrar, Kavi Thakrar and Naved Nasir

~ For carnivores: *Hawksmoor at Home* – Huw Gott, Will Beckett, Richard Turner and Dan Lepard

~ For fusion: *The Moro Cookbook* – Samantha Clark and Samuel Clark

~ For the daring: *The Book of St John* – Fergus Henderson and Trevor Gulliver

~ For rethinking stereotypes: *Mildreds Vegan Cookbook* – Daniel Acevedo and Sarah Wasserman

~ For the coffee table: *The Fat Duck Cookbook* – Heston Blumenthal

# Culture Vulture

## TRY SOMETHING NEW: OPERA

Think of opera as a mash-up of a dramatic performance, live classical music, mind-blowing singing and crazy plotlines. There are highs, lows, baddies and fools. People die, people fall in love. It's funny, dramatic, ludicrous and sad. In fact, often it's not that different to a soap opera.

Things kick off with an overture – a megamix of the best bits of music. Then there will be arias (solo melody) and recitatives (rhythmic talking). There are duets, trios and quartets, and a 'chorus' (a large group of backing singers). You can follow the live line-by-line translation on a screen above the stage (correctly called 'supertitles').

Don't clap until the end of an act, unless there is a particularly impressive moment (a lengthy dying aria, for example). Buffs may shout 'Bravo' or 'Brava'. Applaud when the *maestro* (conductor) takes to the podium, after the interval, after each act and at the end.

Puccini is a good place to start – try *La Bohème* or *Tosca*. There is good music in *La Traviata* by Verdi, or Britten's modern *Peter Grimes*. *The Barber of Seville* by Rossini, or *The Marriage of Figaro* or *The Magic Flute*, both by Mozart, are fun and light.

Bizet's *Carmen* brings Spanish drama or, for politics and power try *Fidelio*, Beethoven's only opera. If the Royal Opera House seems a bit OTT, then look for summer country house opera or opera in the park.

~~~~~~~~~~~~~~~~~~~~~~~~~~~~~~~~~~~~~~~~~~~~~~~~~~~~~~~~~~~~~~~~~

## I KNOW THAT TUNE ... OPERA IN THE MOVIES

~ *A Clockwork Orange* (1971): 'Overture' – *La Gazza Ladra* by Rossini

~ *Apocalypse Now* (1979): 'Ride of the Valkyries' – *Ring Cycle* by Wagner

~ *Fatal Attraction* (1987): 'Un Bel Dì, Vedremo' – *Madame Butterfly* by Puccini

~ *The Untouchables* (1987): 'Vesti la Giubba' – *Pagliacci* by Leoncavallo

~ *The Shawshank Redemption* (1994): 'Sull'aria' – *The Marriage of Figaro* by Mozart

~ *Quantum of Solace* (2008): 'Te Deum' – *Tosca* by Puccini

~ *Mission Impossible: Rogue Nation* (2015): 'Nessun Dorma' – *Turandot* by Puccini (it's also the one Pavarotti sang at the 1990 World Cup)

## STOP THE SHOW: THEATRE CENSORSHIP

Artistic expression has not always been easy. For over 200 years, theatre censorship meant that the Lord Chamberlain had the power to license (or refuse) plays for public viewing. Introduced in 1737 under the Licensing Act, it was an attempt to quash immorality and political satire. The 1968 Theatres Act put an end to restrictions; the next day *Hair* opened in London – the drug-taking, anti-war protests and brief nudity caused shock and delight in equal measure.

## THEATROMANIA: FOUR THEATRICAL FACTS

**Blaze a trail:** Since the Great Fire of London in 1666, no building in the city has been allowed a thatched roof – apart from Shakespeare's Globe.

**Pop shot:** In 1800, there was a failed assassination attempt on King George III in the Theatre Royal, Drury Lane as he stood in the Royal Box during the National Anthem.

**Free spirit:** Until 2016 when *Harry Potter and the Cursed Child* required every seat to be up for grabs, London's Palace Theatre always kept two seats free during performances for the ghosts of an unknown ballerina and Ivor Novello.

**Alter ego:** During the Second World War, Noël Coward ran the British propaganda office in Paris; meanwhile John Gielgud was the fire warden for the Theatre Royal Haymarket during the Blitz.

## SUPERSTITION AND SKULLS

A bit like uttering 'Voldemort' at Hogwarts, it is considered bad luck to say 'Macbeth' in a theatre. Superstitious actors use alternatives such as 'the Scottish play' (unless they are actually performing the Bard's work). On that note, in 1982 Polish composer and pianist André Tchaikowsky bequeathed his skull to the Royal Shakespeare Company but the unusual prop's first outing was not until 1988 in David Tennant's famous parka-wearing performance; previous actors had found using a genuine human remain too chilling.

# Music

## SOUNDTRACK YOUR LIFE

In the age of the curated playlist and algorithmic suggestions, the art of really knowing your music has been viciously eroded, which makes it all the more important to push back against it. Anybody from the age of three and up can log in to their app of choice and dial up a 'feeling happy' playlist, but it's only those in the know who can find an album to perform the same task. Be one of those people. You'll already have some favourites (or should do), so here are some other suggestions …

### Albums to work out to

~ Rage Against the Machine, *Rage Against the Machine* (1992)

~ LCD Soundsystem, *45:33* (2006)

~ Prodigy, *The Fat of the Land* (1997)

### Albums for a Saturday kitchen supper

~ Al Green, *Let's Stay Together* (1972)

~ Bill Evans, *Waltz for Debby* (1962)

~ Guru, *Jazzmatazz, Vol. 1* (1993)

### Albums for a long drive

~ The Jimi Hendrix Experience, *Electric Ladyland* (1968)

~ Rolling Stones, *Let It Bleed* (1969)

~ Tom Petty and The Heartbreakers, *Damn the Torpedoes* (1979)

### Albums for an autumn walk

~ Billie Holiday, *Lady in Satin* (1958)

~ Van Morrison, *Astral Weeks* (1968)

~ Fleet Foxes, *Fleet Foxes* (2008)

### Albums for a summer BBQ

~ Buena Vista Social Club, *Buena Vista Social Club* (1997)

~ Bob Marley and the Wailers, *Exodus* (1977)

~ Groove Armada, *Goodbye Country (Hello Nightclub)* (2001)

### Albums for a cosy roast lunch

~ Ella Fitzgerald and Louis Armstrong, *Ella and Louis* (1956)

~ John Martyn, *Solid Air* (1973)

~ Bob Dylan, *Blood on the Tracks* (1975)

### Albums pre-Friday night down the pub

~ AC/DC, *Back in Black* (1980)

~ Black Keys, *El Camino* (2011)

~ Daft Punk, *Discovery* (2001)

### Albums for late-night company

~ Miles Davis, *Kind of Blue* (1959)

~ Frank Sinatra, *In the Wee Small Hours* (1955)

~ Portishead, *Dummy* (1994)

### Albums for a Sunday morning hangover

~ Aretha Franklin, *Amazing Grace* (1972)

~ Marvin Gaye, *What's Going On* (1971)

~ Nick Drake, *Pink Moon* (1972)

## *Albums to wind down to*

~ The xx, *xx* (2009)

~ Mark Ronson, *Late Night Feelings* (2019)

~ Billy Eilish, *When We All Fall Asleep, Where Do We Go?* (2019)

# Watches

## QUALITY TIME: WHY SPEND MONEY ON A WATCH

Nobody needs a watch anymore. To tell the time, you only have to glance at your computer or phone screen. These days a watch is a luxury item – it should make a statement, whether understated or overstated, and retain a magic that gives you a slight thrill when you glance at your wrist.

## THE SEVEN BASIC TYPES OF WATCH

### *Chronograph*

Any watch with a stopwatch, generally with two or three sub dials and two buttons to start and stop the chronograph. Built for car racing.

~ *Think:* Omega Speedmaster or Rolex Daytona.

### Divers

Built to be water-resistant to at least 100m, legible in total darkness at 25cm and with a rotating bezel to allow you to see how much oxygen is in your tank. And, of course, for pretending to be James Bond.

~ *Think:* Omega Seamaster or Rolex Submariner.

### Pilot

Stylish, casual, detailed for precise timekeeping but often also large, highly visible and rugged. Can be also combined with a chronograph and with dual time functionality.

~ *Think:* IWC or Breitling Aviator.

### Field

Originally designed for soldiers, they are tough, reliable and robust. Built with practicality in mind, the best options are the least complicated.

~ *Think:* Panerai Luminor or Hamilton Khaki.

### Moonphase

Built with a separate dial to track the lunar cycle, moonphases are a magnificent extravagance.

~ *Think:* Patek Philippe or Jaeger-LeCoultre

### Dress

A formal watch, often quite slim, to complement evening wear – or simply a suit and tie. Generally simple, understated, uncomplicated and deliciously elegant.

~ *Think:* Omega De Ville or Montblanc Heritage.

### Smart

A watch devoid of romance, and with the ability to constantly alert you when other people want you. It can play music with poor sound quality, make you feel guilty about not walking far enough and tells you if you're so stressed that you're about to have a heart attack. It's up to you …

# Books

## IT'S NOT ABOUT YOU: AWESOME AUTOBIOGRAPHIES

### Sport

~ *Open: An Autobiography* by Andre Agassi (2009)

~ *Behind the Mask: My Autobiography* by Tyson Fury (2019)

~ *I Am Zlatan* by Zlatan Ibrahimović *(2011)*

~ *Touching the Void* by Joe Simpson (1988)

~ *Proud* by Gareth Thomas (2014)

~ *Coming Back to Me* by Marcus Trescothick (2008)

### Music

~ *Miles: The Autobiography* by Miles Davis (1989)

~ *Chronicles, Vol 1* by Bob Dylan (2004)

~ *Me* by Elton John (2019)

~ *Life* by Keith Richards (2010)

~ *Le Freak* by Nile Rodgers (2011)

~ *Slash*: The Autobiography by Slash (2007)

## Politics

~ *Shortest Way Home* by Pete Buttigieg (2019)

~ *The Blair Years* by Alastair Campbell (2007)

~ *Diaries: In Power* by Alan Clark (1994)

~ *The Alan Johnson Memoirs* (four books) by Alan Johnson (2013–18)

~ *Long Walk to Freedom* by Nelson Mandela (1994)

~ *A Promised Land* by Barack Obama (2020)

## Food

~ *Kitchen Confidential* by Anthony Bourdain (2000)

~ *Heat* by Bill Buford (2006)

~ *The Devil in the Kitchen* by Marco Pierre White (2006)

~ *The Making of a Chef* by Michael Ruhlman (1997)

~ *Toast* by Nigel Slater (2003)

~ *The Man Who Ate Everything* by Jeffrey Steingarten (1997)

## *Celebrity*

~ *Red Carpets and Other Banana Skins* by Rupert Everett (2004)

~ *Bossypants* by Tina Fey (2011)

~ *Stories I Only Tell My Friends* by Rob Lowe (2011)

~ *Born Standing Up* by Steve Martin (2007)

~ *The Moon's a Balloon* by David Niven (1971)

~ *Total Recall: My Unbelievably True Life Story* by Arnold Schwarzenegger (2012)

## *Thought-Provoking*

~ *A Life on Our Planet* by David Attenborough (2020)

~ *In Extremis: The Life of War Correspondent Marie Colvin* by Lindsey Hilsum (2018)

~ *When They Call You a Terrorist* by Patrisse Khan-Cullors and Asha Bandele (2018)

~ *When Breath Becomes Air* by Paul Kalanithi (2016)

~ *H is for Hawk* by Helen Macdonald (2014)

~ *Greenlights* by Matthew McConaughey (2020)

# Driving

## A NOTE ON DRIVING

Whether you're a petrolhead or not, driving is a skill that you will need and should have, so a basic level of competence is vital. Every man should be able to get behind the wheel of a hire car and drive out of a foreign airport with confidence. You should be able to navigate a Cornish single-track lane without brown trousers and at more than 1mph. You should be able to navigate without a sat nav just for your own sense of self-worth.

You should be able to get from one side of a city to another without losing your cool. Reverse parking into a tight spot is not an ancient mystical concept but a basic skill. But mostly, driving is something you should enjoy: a seven-hour road trip is not an endurance mission, but something to relax into with the right music on the stereo, snacks to see you through (and, let's be honest, with iPads packed with film downloads for the kids to watch in the back … unless, of course, you are mad).

'HAVE YOU EVER NOTICED THAT
ANYBODY DRIVING SLOWER THAN
YOU IS AN IDIOT, AND ANYONE GOING
FASTER THAN YOU IS A MANIAC?'

**GEORGE CARLIN**

# Travelling

◆◆———◆◆———◆◆

**LUGGAGE • AIPORTS AND FLYING
PERFECT PROTOCOLS
THE HOUSE GUEST • HOTELS
THE COUNTRY**

'I'VE BEEN TO ALMOST AS MANY
PLACES AS MY LUGGAGE.'

**BOB HOPE**

# Luggage

## MIXED BAG: LUGGAGE ESSENTIALS

Travelling can be stressful at the best of times, so you don't need cranky wheels or cheap zips pushing up your cortisol levels. As you stride through departures, your suitcase should glide behind you on the smoothest of wheels and take the slickest of corners. It should be obedient and move just where you want it with the lightest of touches – dragging and pulling a cheap case is for those destined for Benidorm, not business class.

You will need a suit carrier for, well, when you need your suit. One for business – plain and simple, with lots of pockets – and one for weekends (e.g. a wedding). A carrier that rolls and zips up to look like a duffel bag is a bit more relaxed and car-boot friendly.

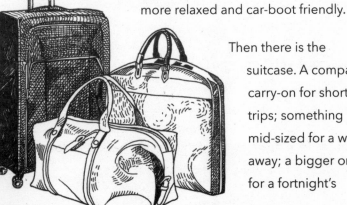

Then there is the suitcase. A compact carry-on for short trips; something mid-sized for a week away; a bigger one for a fortnight's holiday. Make sure they are lightweight to maximise your baggage allowance with what you put inside.

Lastly, the faithful old holdall. A friend for life to accompany you on some of your best times – a weekend in the country, a best mate's wedding, a city break, a quick hotel getaway. Leather will grow old gracefully with character; canvas is more resilient, waterproof and sturdy.

## LIFE SKILL: HOW TO PACK

The best approach is to fill your case Tetris-style with some tactical rolling and folding, and a little bit of stuffing. Put heavier things on the bottom, and items that are prone to creasing nearer the top. If you are after a truly wrinkle-free arrival, then layer items with acid-free tissue paper. Hanging anything creased in a steamy hotel bathroom after a shower can help smooth shirts, trousers and jackets if necessary.

**Shoes:** Place in the bottom of the suitcase, towards the wheels. Make sure they are clean (shoe bags are a good idea) and stuff them with socks. Intersperse smaller items around them, especially in corners and around the edges.

**T-shirts, tops and jumpers:** Lay face down, flip just the sleeves in and roll, full width, from bottom to top, smoothing as you go. Bend the whole roll in half and nestle in your bag.

**Shirts:** Lay face down and fold the sleeves back and down. Fold in half vertically and roll from bottom to top.

**Casual trousers (e.g. chinos and jeans):** Remove belts and empty pockets; fold in half longways and roll from bottom to top.

**Dress / suit trousers:** Butler-style is best for these. Fold lengthways and place half-in / half-out of the suitcase, with the trouser legs hanging over the side. Pack T-shirts, tops and jumpers on top and around them. When you are nearing the top, fold the ends of the trouser legs back into the case, wrapping them around and over the packed clothes.

**Suit jackets / blazers:** Place face down, unbuttoned. Turn the left shoulder inside out, so the inside front of the jacket is lying on the outside back. Fold the right-hand side back (but not inside out) and tuck it inside the fold of the left-hand side. Fold in half lengthways and, if needed to fit in the case, upwards in half again.

**Ties:** Rolled, never folded.

**Underwear:** Rolled or folded, and stuffed into any gaps – it's OK if your smalls get a little creased.

**Washbag:** Place towards the bottom / wheeled end of the case. Keep weight down by using travel-sized products, bag everything up and check for leaky bottles.

🔵FYI *Pack coordinating items that can mix and match. Try applying the three-to-one rule: pack three tops per one pair of bottoms.*

# Airports and Flying

'DID YOU EVER NOTICE THAT
THE FIRST PIECE OF LUGGAGE
ON THE CAROUSEL NEVER
BELONGS TO ANYONE?'

**ERMA BOMBECK**

## FIVE RULES OF FLAWLESS FLYING

### 1. Smooth security

You know the drill: finish your water, bag up your liquids, take off your metals and have your documentation to hand, before you get to the front of the queue. Shame on you if you are the guy self-importantly finding his phone and removing his belt while everyone is waiting for you. It's just rude – and everyone will hate you.

*'An airport is a place where you go through hell to reach your alleged paradise.'* – Stewart Stafford

## 2. Lounge laws

You're not more important than anyone else, so don't behave like you are. Respect the ambience and pre-flight peace. Don't make loud voice calls, monopolise power sockets or watch movies without headphones – and no feet on the seats, ever.

*'Feet off the furniture you Oxbridge t\*\*\*, you're not on a punt now.'* – The Thick of It

## 3. Best behaviour

Once on board, get your baggage in the overhead locker without holding up everyone waiting to get down the aisle. The banned-behaviour list includes encroaching elbows, knees in the back of the seat, antisocial reclining, using another seat to help you stand, armrest hogging and manspreading. If you have a fear of flying, don't be overly dramatic and keep it to yourself …

*'Is there anyone on board who knows how to fly a plane?'* – Airplane

## 4. Keep quiet

Don't inflict conversation on your neighbours or, worse still, try to flirt at 35,000 feet. Keep your own chat with companions at a low volume and make sure other people can't hear your headphones. Unwanted chatty neighbour? Stick on your headphones as a deterrent, even if there's nothing playing.

*'You want to join the mile high club?'* – Crazy/Beautiful

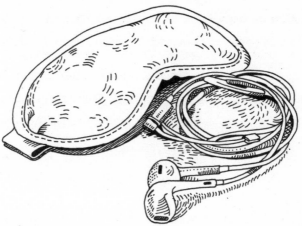

### 5. Child control

If you end up near restless children, try to be understanding if the parents are genuinely doing their best. But if mum and dad are kicking back with a G&T while their toddler is jumping on the seats, feel free to pass judgement. If it's your kids running riot, then get involved – in-flight movies and noise-cancelling headphones are for solo trips.

*'No matter which kid's book I read to my screaming baby on an airplane, the moral of the story is always something about a vasectomy.' – Ryan Reynolds*

## STYLE IT OUT: IN-FLIGHT FASHION

Comfort is key at 35,000 feet, but there is no need to let your usual standards slip. You don't want to be checking into your hotel in a tracksuit, so leave the loungewear at home. Aim to step off the plane and be comfortable in the climate, but that doesn't mean travelling in your beach shorts; your holiday wardrobe can wait until you have a room number. Wear shoes that are easy to get on and off for security and on-board ease (but don't even consider flip-flops) and never go barefoot in the cabin.

**FYI** *Free up luggage space and weight allowance by wearing /taking the biggest item on the plane, for example a coat or chunky jumper.*

---

'FLYING FIRST CLASS MEANS SITTING NEXT TO A BETTER CLASS OF PERSON I DON'T WANT TO TALK TO.'

**DOV DAVIDOFF**

---

## IN THE KNOW: UPGRADES

**There are a few tricks that might help you to turn left when you board …**

~ You may have enough miles to upgrade yourself. Lie back and reap the benefits – you earnt it after all.

~ It doesn't always take two to tango. Solo travellers are offered upgrades to fill a spare seat, whereas it's rare for couples and never going to happen for groups. If you're on your own, offer to be bumped off a busy flight – but secure that upgrade first.

~   Look slovenly and you won't fit the bill; it really can be as
    simple as dressing the part.

~   Good things come to those who are nice. You will never
    seem deserving of a lie-flat bed if you aren't pleasant to
    everyone with the upgrade powers.

# Perfect Protocols

'TRAVEL IS ABOUT THE
GORGEOUS FEELING OF
TEETERING IN THE UNKNOWN.'

**ANTHONY BOURDAIN**

## KEEP THE CHANGE: TOP TIPS

Inconveniently, there is no international standard when it comes to tipping. While you don't tip taxis in Beijing, Singapore, Hong Kong, Mumbai or Dubai, you are expected to give 10% in Johannesburg and Paris. Tipping a cabbie in Tokyo would cause offence; in Istanbul, Madrid, Stockholm and Sydney it's customary to round up to the nearest unit, but drivers in New York and LA would expect to see an extra 15–20% on their fare. Confused? Even the most seasoned traveller should research the going rate at their destination to avoid any cross-cultural offence.

Nonchalantly pressing notes into palms doesn't come naturally to most of us, especially the British who have always had an awkward relationship with tipping. In the UK today, there is the National Minimum Wage and wages cannot be topped up by tips, so think of it as both a one-off acknowledgement of good service, and a way of future-proofing good service with people who you see regularly.

In day-to-day British life, there are only a few tips you need to remember. For a regular taxi ride, round up to the nearest pound, but if the cabbie has gone the extra mile add 10-15%. In restaurants, service is often included, so check when paying or add 10-15%. The going rate for hairdressers and barbers is around 10% – give a decent tip after each cut to ensure you look great after your next visit too. (For hotels, see p.205).

'THIS CERTIFIES THAT YOU HAVE HAD A PERSONAL ENCOUNTER WITH ME AND THAT YOU FOUND ME WARM, POLITE, INTELLIGENT AND FUNNY'

**PRINTED ON COMEDIAN STEVE MARTIN'S BUSINESS CARDS**

## INTERNATIONAL BUSINESS CARD ETIQUETTE

When you are giving out your business card overseas, it can be useful to have one side translated into the recipient's native language. Avoid embarrassing mistakes and use an expert translator, rather than a friend who claims fluency. You only need to include your name, position/job title, company name and contact details. If your job title is complicated, then simplify it without diminishing your status.

In the Western world, there is little ceremony around the exchange of business cards. Keep your cards in good condition in a card holder, and while you don't need to show too much reverence when you receive other people's cards, do treat them with a little respect. Never give out your card in a social setting.

Many other regions place great importance on the exchange of business cards, and they are symbols of respect, camaraderie and status. Be sure to get your business trip off to a flying start with some etiquette know-how for exchanging cards …

### Japan: expect some ceremony

Present your card with the translated text facing the recipient; it is best to use both hands. Bow lightly and say your name and your job title. Always receive a card with both hands; hold it below chest-level and examine it carefully. In a meeting, place the card on the table in front of you – you will receive cards from everyone present in hierarchical order, starting with the most senior person. If you are standing, place the card in a card holder; never just stick it in your pocket.

### China: translation is key

Make sure your card is translated accurately: in mainland China and Singapore you should use 'simplified' characters, whereas in Taiwan and areas of Hong Kong it is correct to use 'traditional' characters. Present your card with two hands, with the translated text facing the recipient. Receive their card with two hands and spend some time studying it. Again, place it in a card holder, never in your pocket.

### Middle East: right is right

It is a good idea to have one side of your card translated into Arabic. Business cards are exchanged straight after introductions; present yours with either two hands or with your right hand (never your left) and receive cards in the same way. If you are in a meeting, place any cards you have received in front of you.

### India: academic accolades

There is no need to have your card translated, but academic achievements are highly respected in India so include any degrees or honours. There isn't much ceremony around giving and receiving, but only use your right hand.

# The House Guest

## BE MY GUEST: HOUSE GUEST RULES

Staying at other people's houses is an etiquette minefield, no matter how well you know them. Every household has their own way of doing things – your job is to fit in, while being fun and fuss-free.

**All the gear, right idea:** Don't arrive in the countryside with just lightweight trainers and no warm coat; think about where you are going, and what you might be doing. Don't be shy: find out what is planned and what you need to bring.

**Bear gifts:** Never show up empty-handed. The usual options are a bottle of fizz (bonus points if you arrive with it chilled), chocolates (go luxury), candles (nothing too smelly), flowers (not from the garage) and wine (be generous). Take something for their kids – depending on their age, comics and sticker books are safe options, and may be more popular with the parents than sweets.

**When in Rome:** Live by their timings and fit in. Children's schedules can easily collide; relax the routine for a couple of nights or you risk your kids' needs anti-socially hijacking everyone's plans. Read the signs for yourself too – don't be holding court and asking for more wine in the early hours if your hosts are drinking tea and turning off the lights.

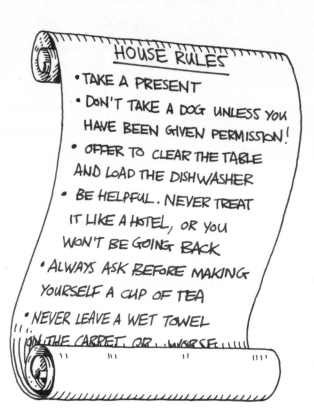

HOUSE RULES
- TAKE A PRESENT
- DON'T TAKE A DOG UNLESS YOU HAVE BEEN GIVEN PERMISSION!
- OFFER TO CLEAR THE TABLE AND LOAD THE DISHWASHER
- BE HELPFUL. NEVER TREAT IT LIKE A HOTEL, OR YOU WON'T BE GOING BACK
- ALWAYS ASK BEFORE MAKING YOURSELF A CUP OF TEA
- NEVER LEAVE A WET TOWEL ON THE CARPET OR, WORSE

———•——••——•———

## 'NO GUEST IS SO WELCOME IN A FRIEND'S HOUSE THAT HE WILL NOT BECOME A NUISANCE AFTER THREE DAYS.'

**PLAUTUS**

———•——••——•———

**Do your bit:** Offer to clear the table, wash up or chop some vegetables. Don't unload the dishwasher (you don't know where it all goes) or offer to lay the table (you don't know where everything is). And if your host's culinary skills fill you with horror, don't muscle in, take over the stove or pass critical comment.

**Respect the boundaries:** Open the curtains, make the bed and hang up your towel. Don't hog the bathroom, don't leave any mess around. Clear up after your children. Respect any shoes-off rule. Ask before making a cup of tea, helping yourself from the fridge or pouring yourself a glass from the bottle – even if you know your hosts really well it is surprisingly easy to be irritatingly intrusive.

**Say thank you:** For longer stays, say three nights or more, try to take everyone out for a meal – pub lunch or similar – and foot the bill. When you get home, also follow up with a thank you.

# Hotels

## FIVE-STAR BEHAVIOUR: HOTEL ETIQUETTE

When it comes to five-star service, there are three types of customer: the wealthy or famous who live it full-time; the business person who wants it for efficiency and ease; the honeymooners or experience-seekers who are treating themselves to something special. Whichever you are, there are ways of living the luxury lifestyle …

~ You don't need to strut your stuff in a three-piece, but wandering around in swimming trunks or loungewear won't cut it. Go for relaxed smart casual in public areas – decent jeans, tailored shorts, a collar – and check out the dress code for the restaurant. You may never want to leave your room again if you pitch up for your table in shorts and T-shirt, to be met by a sea of pressed pastel linen.

~ You're not a backpacker. Don't talk loudly in your room or in echoey corridors, particularly late at night and early in the morning; keep television and music volume levels down; don't let doors slam. Rushing around noisily is not five-star behaviour.

~ If you have your children with you, don't let them run riot like it's a family-friendly all-inclusive. If you bring your little angels, you need to do some parenting (or give them to someone else to deal with – cue kids' club).

~ Luxury hotels often attract famous faces – don't stare (or worse, point). A quick smile of recognition is fine but stopping an A-lister for a selfie is just embarrassing (for you) and annoying (for them).

~ Don't succumb to slob-like standards: put rubbish in the bin, make the bed, open the curtains, pick up clothes, pile dirty towels in one place in the bathroom. You're not a teenager on a messy week in Magaluf.

~ The best service comes to those who remember their pleases and thank-yous, and if something isn't up to scratch, charm rather than aggression will get better results.

~ Go to the concierge before you start googling – they are some of the best-connected people around and it's their job to get you access to all the hard-to-get tickets and tables.

~ While a few of the little bottles of complimentary shower gel might find their way home with you, the same doesn't go for dressing gowns, or small fixtures and fittings. And breakfast is breakfast; don't fill your pockets to keep yourself going during the day. If you can afford a five-star room, you can afford to buy lunch.

~ Tip properly. For porters in British hotels, it's £1 per bag on check-in and check-out. Give a small note to concierges and doormen if they are particularly helpful; leave housekeeping around £2 per day. You can leave something larger for everyone at the end of your stay, but tipping as you go usually oils the wheels of excellent service.

'LIVING IN THE LAP OF LUXURY ISN'T BAD,
EXCEPT THAT YOU NEVER KNOW WHEN
LUXURY IS GOING TO STAND UP.'

**ORSON WELLES**

## THE BRIGHT LIGHTS OF LUXURY

Aiming to beat the basic standards of British hospitality
and emulate the glamour of American hotels, the first
luxury hotel in London was The Savoy, which opened its
doors in 1889. Its use of electricity throughout the hotel
was groundbreaking: guests had their own light switches
in their rooms. Electric lifts, known as 'ascending rooms',
were installed and there were speaking tubes for guests
to summon maids and valets. Most forward-thinking of all,
it was the first hotel to introduce en suite bathrooms with
(very un-British) cascading showers.

# The Country

## RURAL RULES

~ Stick to footpaths, leave gates as you found them (usually shut), keep your dog on a lead in villages, on lanes and farmland, and check if they are welcome in the pub.

~ Drive slowly on narrow lanes, be prepared to reverse, give way to oncoming cars going uphill and keep your hand off the horn.

~ Say 'good morning' and 'good afternoon' (even if they are strangers) and be prepared to stop for a (often mindless) chat. It really can be just like *The Archers*.

~ Don't dress in stylised country gear and top-to-toe tweed – dress for the weather and wear sensible shoes.

## IN THE KNOW: THE COUNTRY WEEKEND

The country weekend comes with its own set of rules. For insiders, the gentle rhythm and requirements of rural hospitality are second nature but, if you are new to it all, good preparation and research will prevent any etiquette faux pas.

### What to Wear

Take proper shoes. You need something sturdy but casual (like a leather boot), something smart but casual (a brown Derby fits the bill) and a decent pair of wellingtons (in a muted colour, not clean or bright green). Leave the trainers at home.

The evening is likely to be smart casual (never take your suit). Think chinos, an Oxford shirt and a blazer, and layer with a merino jumper – it's likely to be on the chilly side. In warmer weather, a classic linen shirt and chinos looks the part for a Pimm's in the garden. If your hosts are properly old-school, then 'dressing for dinner' may mean black tie. Check in advance.

Seasoned country-dwellers seem immune to the cold because they wear proper gear. This is not the time for a bum-freezing bomber – a waxed jacket (Barbour or similar) is versatile, warm and waterproof, and everyone will most likely be wearing one. For warmer weather, a classic field jacket works well.

And pack it all in a weekend holdall, preferably battered leather; suitcases on wheels are for city hotels and airports.

### Things to Consider

Check what you are doing in advance. Aside from the usual country gear, you might need swimming or tennis things if there is a pool or court. It never feels very grown-up if you have to ask to borrow.

Don't act like you are in *Downton Abbey*. If you find yourself parking outside a small stately home on the Friday night, avoid

assuming unnatural airs and graces. Take it all in your stride
– the traditional British upper classes are underwhelmed by
nearly everything (but that doesn't mean be unappreciative).

You may find yourself off-grid. Mobile phone reception can be
patchy and Wi-Fi signals weak. Never complain and don't ask
for network passwords as soon as you arrive – the slower pace
of life means checking your inbox less.

Be a good sport. Whether it's a flutter at the races, a game
of croquet on the lawn or a quick tennis match, don't get too
competitive and be good-humoured (even if you are struggling
to see the funny side).

While the champagne may have been popped early and the
port still doing the rounds late into the evening, you will still
have an early start so pace yourself. Luckily, the outdoors does
wonders for a hangover – something a true country gent will
never admit to, no matter how grim he feels.

'THE CUP OF TEA ON ARRIVAL AT A
COUNTRY HOUSE IS A THING WHICH,
AS A RULE, I PARTICULARLY ENJOY.
I LIKE THE CRACKLING LOGS, THE
SHADED LIGHTS, THE SCENT OF
BUTTERED TOAST, THE GENERAL
ATMOSPHERE OF LEISURED COSINESS.'

**P.G. WODEHOUSE**

# Sport

FITNESS • SPORTING PROWESS
SPECTATING • HORSERACING
SPORTING SOCIETY

'ONE MAN PRACTISING
SPORTSMANSHIP IS FAR
BETTER THAN FIFTY
PREACHING IT.'

KNUTE ROCKNE

# Fitness

## WHY EXERCISE

There are mountains of scientific evidence as to why leading a more active life makes you happier, healthier and, frankly, less likely to die. You'll have heard the arguments a thousand times, and if they haven't got you exercising yet, then repeating them here isn't going to change your mind.

But there is one thing to consider: exercise is the best way to start looking better than the bloke who sits next to you in the office or opposite you on the train. And that's how you start standing out. Have a better shirt than him, a better haircut and, underneath all that, a better, firmer body. The secret confidence that will give you is a powerful thing.

'MUSCLES ... THEY'RE LIKE PETS AND THEY'RE NOT WORTH IT ... YOU HAVE TO FEED THEM ALL THE TIME AND TAKE CARE OF THEM, AND IF YOU DON'T, THEY JUST GO AWAY. THEY RUN AWAY.'

**RYAN GOSLING**

## EIGHT RULES OF THE GYM

1.  *Towel down.* Clean up after yourself – wipe down the machines and equipment (with your own towel). Even if you didn't sweat, it's what's expected.

2.  *Clock watching.* Don't hog the machines or ignore people who are waiting.

3.  *Freshen up.* Make sure your kit makes its way into the washing machine, rather than festering in your gym bag for weeks. After all, people are working out and breathing deeply.

4.  *Drowned out.* Your motivating soundtrack is designed just for you, not to be broadcast via your tinny headphones.

5.  *Power dressing.* Keep your shirt on and your clothes modest.

6.  *Tidy up.* Just as you were taught to put your toys away, if you use something, put it back.

7.  *Self-reliant.* Your workout is your workout. Do it for yourself, not to impress others. They really aren't interested.

8.  *The silent treatment:* Don't chat to strangers; don't pass comment on others' workouts; don't disturb others by chattering to friends. You're there to sweat, not socialise.

## FIVE RULES OF THE POOL

1.  Don't pick a lane you can't keep up with.

2.  Obey the one-way system when doing your lengths.

3.  Allow people to overtake if you are lagging behind.

4.  Only swim single file.

5.  Don't stare.

## HOME RUN: ESSENTIAL WORKOUT GEAR

**Shorts:** Flexible and non-chafing. A Lycra underlayer wards off any peekaboo issues. In colder weather, opt for Lycra trousers instead of heavier tracksuit trousers.

**T-shirt:** Loose or flexible, in a material that wicks sweat from the body. Try adding a thermal base layer in winter.

**Dry-fit jacket:** Whether long-sleeved or a gilet, it should be sweat-wicking, waterproof and with plenty of ventilation so you don't turn into a sweaty, boil-in the-bag mess.

**Proper trainers:** Running shoes are built for running in, and specialist running shops can analyse your gait and running style – a good idea before you attempt a new personal best. Cross-training shoes are more versatile, and are fine for aerobics or other classes, as well as lifting weights.

**Heart rate monitor / smart phone or watch:** Essential for performance monitoring. Keep up with where your limits are, and where you can push them further.

---

### WARTIME RULES OF GOLF

In the autumn of 1940, during The Blitz, a bomb fell on an outbuilding belonging to Richmond Golf Club in Surrey, prompting the club to issue a set of temporary wartime rules. Here are some highlights:

~ 'In Competitions, during gunfire or while bombs are falling, players may take cover without penalty for ceasing play.'

~ 'A player whose stroke is affected by the simultaneous explosion of a bomb may play another ball from the same place. Penalty one stroke.'

~ 'Players are asked to collect bomb and shrapnel splinters to save these causing damage to the mowing machines.'

## ON SCREEN: BOND ON SKIS

*On Her Majesty's Secret Service* (1969) – Mürren, Switzerland. The one where he escapes Blofeld's mountain top HQ and is chased down the mountain, ending up on just one ski.

*The Spy Who Loved Me* (1977) – St Moritz, Switzerland. The one where he throws himself off a cliff and launches a Union Jack parachute, while wearing a banana-yellow snowsuit.

*For Your Eyes Only* (1981) – Cortina d'Ampezzo, Italy. The one where he takes on a ski jump, goes down a bobsleigh track and glides through a restaurant, all while being chased by motorbikes.

*A View to A Kill* (1985) – St Moritz, Switzerland. The one where he escapes on a snowboard fashioned from a piece of snowmobile (to the Beach Boys).

*The Living Daylights* (1987) – Bratislava, Slovakia. The one where he and his Bond girl 'ski' on her cello case and cross the Austrian border.

*The World Is Not Enough* (1999) – Chamonix, France. The one where he out-skis and brings down machine-gun-wielding snow-mobile paragliders.

# Sporting Prowess

*Master a few tricks to perform like a pro (or just impress your mates) …*

### Cricket: How to bowl leg spin

1. Grip the ball between first and second finger, across the seam, and resting on thumb and third finger. It should not be too tight, nor too loose.

2. Use your bowling action to increase the spin – approach the crease almost with your shoulder towards the batsman, then pivot sharply in your delivery stride. Aim the seam towards where the first slip would stand for a right-hander.

3. Bowl the ball with the back of the hand towards you and twist your wrist as you release it – imagine you are opening a round door handle – and using the third and fourth finger to impart extra revs. The palm should be facing upwards after release.

4. Aim for the right-handed batsman's leg stump, or just outside, with the intention of turning the ball past the off stump.

5. Blond hair highlights, *à la* Shane Warne, optional.

### Rugby: How to kick a spiral punt

1. Hold the ball waist-high, one hand on top and one hand underneath.

2. Point the ball slightly downwards, and away from you (right-footers: point down and to the left; left-footers: down and to the right).

3. Bring the ball up to shoulder height, and then down – moving the bottom hand away as it falls.

4. Point your toes and kick through the ball in a straight line at the target, allowing the ball to roll off the top of the foot as you connect.

5. Follow through fully for maximum distance, and to discourage any on-rushing flankers from getting too close.

### Football: How to do the Cruyff turn

1. Position the ball slightly in front of you, as if to play a pass.

2. Swing your leg forward, as if passing or shooting, but then hook your foot around the front of the ball and scoop the ball backwards behind you.

3.  Swivel your body as swiftly as possible so that you are facing in the opposite direction.

4.  Sprint off with the ball, but turn briefly to check for a defender on his back flicking the V's at you.

### Golf: How to create backspin on pitch shots

1.  Choose a 54–58 degree wedge; make sure it is clean with hard grooves. Choose a soft-core, rather than a hard-core, ball.

2.  Hit from a reasonable distance – backspin requires the ball to be hit at speed, so will be far easier at 80–90 yards than 10–20. Hitting into the breeze on a soft green will help too.

3.  Adopt a narrow stance with the ball in the middle, and with hands neither behind nor in front of the ball. A touch of weight on the lead foot can help.

4.  Aim to take a very shallow divot as you strike the ball and hit it hard with an even swing.

5.  Curse as the ball spins so far it rolls off the front of the green.

### Cycling: How to do a bunny hop

1.  Pull up the front wheel of the bike, as if doing a wheelie.

2.  As the front wheel comes up, lean forward and push your handlebars forward too.

3. Flick the back off the ground at the same time.

4. Make sure bits and pieces are out of the way as you land back on your seat, unless you want to walk cross-legged for the rest of the day.

### Workout: How to do the perfect press-up

1. Get into a high plank: hands on the floor under the shoulder blades, fingers facing forwards, toes pushed into the ground for stability. Brace your core and flatten your back.

2. With back still flat, bum level and eyes looking forwards, lower your body while breathing in until the chest brushes the floor. Maintain a straight line from neck to toe.

3. Push back up into starting position while breathing out, with body still in a straight line.

4. Avoid sagging, back arching and head-dipping, and try not to let arms flare out sideways.

5. Repeat until ripped.

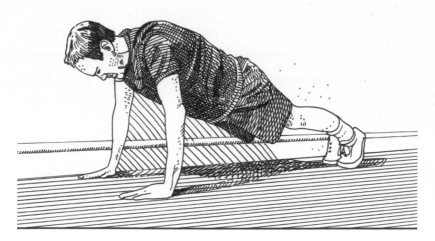

## THE PRINCIPLE OF SPORTSMANSHIP

Everyone knows the principals of good sportsmanship – losing well, winning with grace, respect for the game, blah, blah, blah – but there is a more valid point in play. Everyone who has ever played sport has, at some point, seen a member of the opposition lose the run of themselves: yelling, swearing and throwing stuff in defeat or bragging, boasting and jeering in victory. And everyone has had the same thought: 'T*sser'. So, you can click on all the motivational blogs on sportsmanship, listen to all the podcasts on the spirit of the game, and read all the books on ethical behaviour but, really, good sportsmanship comes down to one thing: don't be that t*sser.

'I HATED EVERY MINUTE OF TRAINING, BUT I SAID, "DON'T QUIT. SUFFER NOW AND LIVE THE REST OF YOUR LIFE AS A CHAMPION".'

**MUHAMMAD ALI**

# Spectating

*What to say to keep up with the crowd.*

*Cricket*

**Don't say:** 'Not much is happening.'
**Do say:** 'Fascinating tactical battle.'

**Don't say:** 'Why are they stopping again?'
**Do say:** 'It'll be interesting to see if they change their approach in the next session.'

**Don't say:** 'When does this bloody end?'
**Do say:** 'A five-day Test match is the ultimate challenge of technique.'

**Don't say:** 'The gardening is really impressive.'
**Do say:** 'Looks like a green wicket, one for the seamers rather than the spinners.'

**Don't say:** 'He keeps missing the ball.'
**Do say:** 'He's leaving well, really pacing his innings.'

### Rugby

**Don't say:** 'It's a bit rough – is it basically just a massive punch-up?'
**Do say:** 'It'll be key to see who dominates the breakdown – that's where the game will be won.'

**Don't say:** 'It's just a pile of bodies, it's impossible to see what's going on.'
**Do say:** 'The forwards are controlling the game.'

**Don't say:** 'How do they get anywhere if they keep passing it backwards.'
**Do say:** 'Wonderful kicking game from the fly-half / full-back.'

**Don't say:** 'Who are the fat blokes in the scrum? And what happens when they meet the scrawny guys at the back?'
**Do say:** 'Rugby is the ultimate game for everyone, of all sizes.'

**Don't say:** 'Why is that bloke sticking his head in the other guy's bum?'
**Do say:** 'Watch the binding from the second row – could be crucial for scrum stability.'

### Football

**Don't say:** 'Why do they keep throwing themselves to the ground.'
**Do say:** 'Modern referees just don't give fouls unless a player really makes the most of it – it's a vicious circle.'

**Don't say:** 'Why do they keep stopping to look at the TV?'
**Do say:** 'VAR is ruining the game.'

**Don't say:** 'You know what, I don't actually mind who wins.'
**Do say:** 'The other team are a bunch of t*ssers.'

**Don't say:** 'It's just a bunch of people kicking a ball – it's hardly important.'
**Do say:** 'Some people think football is a matter of life and death – I can assure you, it's more important than that.'

**Don't say:** 'Now that they've had two players sent off and are three goals down, I think we can relax.'
**Do say:** 'I still reckon we can lose this from here if we're not careful.'

# Horseracing

## I AM YOUR FATHER: THOROUGHBREDS

The ancestry of every thoroughbred horse born in Britain
(and nearly all around the world) can be traced through the
father's bloodline back to one of three sires, brought back to
Britain from Africa and the Middle East in the seventeenth and
eighteenth centuries: the Byerley Turk, the Darley Arabian and
the Godolphin Arabian.

## TYPES OF RACING

Jump racing (also called National Hunt racing) is racing with
hurdles and steeplechase fences (which can include water and
ditches). The main season is from late October until April, when
the ground is softer. The best-known meetings are the Grand
National and Cheltenham Festival.

Flat racing, funnily enough, is racing with no jumps, run over a
set distance. The ground needs to be firm (for speed), so the
season runs over drier months, largely May until October. It's
more glamorous than jump racing; the prize money is greater
and the big meetings have smart dress codes and high-society
links – famous examples include the Epsom Derby, Royal Ascot
and Glorious Goodwood.

## HOW TO BACK A WINNER

*It's estimated that the favourite only wins 30% of the time, so it can pay to study the form. Don't get carried away – seeing your horse heading for the winning post can really get the adrenaline pumping, but remember that the house always wins in the end.*

**Winning streak:** Look for horses that have recently won a few races in a row or, even if they didn't win, have recently achieved a personal best. Conversely, a horse that has run badly due to conditions may perform better on a different day; a horse that is fresh from a rest may be ready for a good race.

**Track record:** Achieved at Ascot? Champion at Cheltenham? Trainers, jockeys and horses all have preferred courses. Look at where they have done well (and less well) as it is safe to assume they may pull it out of the bag again.

**Best in class:** Look at the class of horses, then check what class your horse was previously. If it has dropped a class, it may well still have the edge over lower-class runners.

**Surface tension:** Some horses suit firm (dry) conditions, and vice versa. Check what the 'going' (ground conditions) was like last time they won or ran well. If current conditions don't match, they might not be the right choice for now.

## ODDS ON: HOW TO CALCULATE YOUR WINNINGS

There is a simple formula to work out your 'return' (winnings) on single bets: divide the first number by the second, plus your stake. For example, in very simple terms, if you bet £1 on a horse with 2-1 odds, you would stand to win £2, plus the £1 stake, so a total of £3; bet £1 on a 16-2 horse, and you would stand to win £8, plus the £1 stake, so £9.

Betting each way is more complicated, and depends how many runners are in the field, but essentially you are betting on a win, plus a second, third or, sometimes, fourth place. You need to put down twice the stake as half is for the bet to win, and the other half for the place. If you win, you get the return for the win and the place, so you can do very well. Remember, though, if you bet each way on a horse with odds of less than 5-1, you may come out with less than what you initially put down. Not very cool.

# Sporting Society

*Sport isn't all about sweating it out – here's how the other half get their sporting fix.*

---

## ETIQUETTE SOS: SHOOTING

*Game shooting may no longer be the preserve of the upper classes, but every shoot comes with a strict set of rules and etiquette. Do your research and be prepared – not only to fit in, but also to stay safe.*

**Answer the call:** If you are invited to go game shooting (pheasant, partridge, grouse, etc.) then reply quickly. It's not the time to be cool and hang back; your host needs to establish numbers.

**Booster shot:** Learn the ropes or brush up with a few lessons from a shooting school. Never pretend to your host that you are more experienced than you are – firing at a few clays is very different to standing alongside a seasoned gun in the field.

**All set:** Being late for a shoot is the height of bad manners. Before you get going, there will be a briefing that will cover the format of the day, safety advice and a draw of pegs (where you will stand to shoot for each drive). Listen carefully.

**Sporting times:** No stealing or poaching of other people's birds; no bragging or boasting about a good shot. No leaving early, whatever the weather; phones stay put away and on silent. Carry your gun unloaded in a sleeve or broken over your arm.

**Hunger games:** You may break for lunch, or wait until later after finishing shooting. Sometimes it's laid on, sometimes it's bring your own. There will be a refuel mid-morning – take along some sloe gin to share around.

**At your service:** It is essential that you tip the gamekeeper. The average rate is £20–30 per 100 birds and £10 for every hundred after that, but check with your host. Give them cash at the end of the day – like an American bellboy, they will be expecting it.

**Follow up:** Put pen to paper and write your host a thank-you letter. It's not old-fashioned – it's good form.

## HOT SHOT: WHAT TO WEAR

Shooting clothes should be practical for the weather and always muted in colour (greens, browns, etc.). There is no need for proper tweed, but everything should be warm and waterproof. Never wear jeans, but always wear a proper shirt and tie – turn up open-necked and you'll receive looks that will make you get straight back in your car and drive home. Wear wellies or hiking boots, gloves and a tweed flat cap. You also need ear defenders, a gun slip, cartridge bag and (often) your own cartridges.

∗────∗────∗

## 'I NEVER KNOW WHICH IS WORSE: THE SORROW WHEN YOU HIT THE BIRD OR THE SHAME WHEN YOU MISS IT.'

**JULIAN FELLOWES**

∗────∗────∗

## AHOY THERE: YACHT BEHAVIOUR

*Yachting may say high life, but it comes with plenty of etiquette and passenger expectation. Play by the rules or cabin fever may quickly set in.*

~ Pack light, in a soft holdall, and be prepared for the weather. Pack your sunscreen, swimmers and sunnies; stick in a warm jumper and sporty waterproof jacket. Shirts and shorts / casual chinos are the perfect combo for covering up in the sun and looking smooth with a sundowner.

~ Arrive in soft-soled deck shoes or trainers; once on board you'll most likely be barefoot.

~ Ask to board by saying, 'May I come aboard please?'. It's the done thing.

~ Boats are expensive, and it's likely to be the owner's pride and joy. Be suitably impressed.

~ Remember that yachting is essentially posh camping. Cabins are small, so keep it tidy; water is limited, so be sparing; loos ('heads') are prone to blocking, so go carefully.

~ The captain's word is final. He may be an old mate on dry land, but he's the skipper at sea, and that comes with responsibility for the boat and everyone's safety.

~ Sailing is more involved than it looks. Larking about won't raise any laughs.

~ If you're lucky enough to be on board a bigger yacht with a crew, let them get on with their jobs, respect their quarters and privacy, and remember to tip them at the end.

---

**POSH: PORT OUT, STARBOARD HOME**

It's widely accepted that 'posh' is an anacronym that identified the best cabins in the steamships that went between Britain and India. On the way out, port-side cabins got the morning sun and cooled off during the rest of the day, and the reverse was true on the way home. Essentially, you paid to keep cool.

---

## HIGH SOCIETY: THE SEASON

The Season was once a string of exclusive social events that helped the upper classes stick together and ensure their children married each other. Today, it is a mix of socialite scene, international wealth and corporate hospitality, with some of the old school hanging in there to keep up tradition. There are a few things that unify the key events: the kudos of a badge for the best enclosure, a strict dress code, plenty of booze and a fancy car picnic, whatever the weather. Best of British.

––––– •• –––––

'OH! TALK TO EVERY WOMAN AS IF YOU LOVED HER, AND TO EVERY MAN AS IF HE BORED YOU, AND AT THE END OF YOUR FIRST SEASON YOU WILL HAVE THE REPUTATION OF POSSESSING THE MOST PERFECT SOCIAL TACT.'

**OSCAR WILDE,** *A WOMAN OF NO IMPORTANCE*

––––– •• –––––

### *Henley Royal Regatta*

~ *What is it?* A five-day rowing regatta in late June / early July.

~ *What's the fuss?* For the rowing world, it's a high-profile event; for socialites, it's a chance to drink Pimm's by the river and get dressed up.

~ *Sporting highlights?* The Grand Challenge Cup for Men's Eights is the most famous race.

~ *Where to be seen?* The Stewards' Enclosure. Two big grandstands with the best view. You need to be invited in by a member (the waiting list is over five years) and you must wear a suit, or blazer and chinos, and a tie (if you have one from a public school of note, this is the time to dust if off and indulge in the old boys' club). The dress code is rigorously enforced, as is the no mobile phone policy – make or take a call and you will be escorted out.

~ *What else happens?* A picnic at the car. Pack table and chairs; upgrade the Tupperware for proper china and glasses; chill a bottle of decent fizz; prepare the poshest of picnic lunches.

~ *Sound like a pro:* All races are rowed two abreast – crews are assigned either 'Berks' (Berkshire, towpath side) or 'Bucks' (Buckinghamshire) side.

~ *Seasonal fool:* Never wear a rowing blazer unless you've earnt it. There is a code of recognition among the rowing world; wearing a shop-bought replica will have you laughed off the towpath.

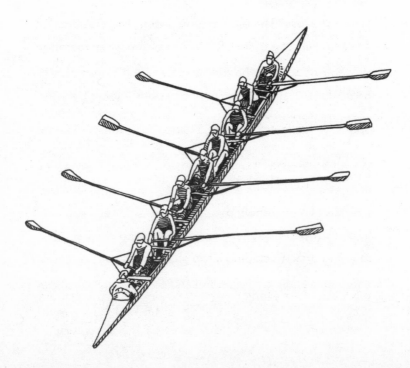

'WINNING A ROWING RACE IS NOT LIKE WINNING ANYTHING ELSE. HERE'S MY THEORY: YOU'RE FACING BACKWARDS, SO YOU'RE LOOKING AT THE PEOPLE YOU'RE BEATING – AND THERE'S SOMETHING EXQUISITE ABOUT THAT.'

**HUGH LAURIE**

### *Royal Ascot*

~ *What is it?* World-class racing; high-class fashion; lots of royalty.

~ *What's the fuss?* The buzz around Ladies' Day (Thursday) and the daily two o'clock Royal Procession when members of the Royal Family, and their guests, arrive from Windsor Castle in open-topped carriages.

~ *Sporting highlights?* Thursday's Gold Cup is the most famous.

~ *Where to be seen?* The Royal Enclosure. No riff-raff here, it's the most exclusive area. The best views come with the strictest of entry requirements and dress codes – you need to be the guest of a member, and you need to wear full morning dress (including a top hat; shoes must be black).

~ *What else does everyone do?* If you don't book a restaurant, then it's the posh car picnic (see Henley).

~ *Sound like a pro:* Comment on the famous 73-foot climb from Swinley Bottom up to the Winning Post.

~ *Seasonal fool:* Get your morning dress details on the mark – no wing collars or oversized cravats (see p.56), or you look like you've stepped out of a hire shop. Not the done thing.

## Glorious Goodwood

~ *What is it?* A five-day race meeting, set in the Sussex countryside.

~ *What's the fuss?* Once described by King Edward VII as 'a garden party with racing tacked on', it's smart but relaxed fun – and the racecourse is beautiful.

~ *Sporting highlights?* The Sussex Stakes is one to watch.

~ *Where to be seen?* The Richmond Enclosure is the swankiest; you need to be in a jacket and tie.

~ *What else does everyone do?* Another posh car picnic, a flutter and lots of fizz.

~ *Sound like a pro:* Recollect how the Sussex Stakes is the only race that Frankel competed in, and won, twice (2011 and 2012).

~ *Seasonal fool:* A panama is the order of the day. Don't get muddled with a fedora – it's the summer, so stick to straw.

'ONE WORD OF ADVICE:
AVOID THE STEAMING DIVOT!'

*PRETTY WOMAN*

## IN THE KNOW: POLO

**The royal treatment:** Polo is also one of the world's oldest sports, dating back to 600 BC in Persia, but today's version is the result of adaptations made by nineteenth-century British army officers. The royal connections have made polo the stuff of aspirational high society, helped by young British princes thundering around the field, but a day at the polo is a relaxed and quintessentially British affair.

**Dress code:** Classic smart casual. Chinos, shirt, blazer, with a country garden-party vibe: brown shoes, pastel shirt and linen or light fabrics. If it's corporate hospitality, you might need a suit, but only if it's the most formal kind, and at a really big match. Sunglasses are a must; if the weather is unpredictable stick a wax jacket or similar in the car.

**Game time:** Until you watch live polo, it is hard to get an idea of the size, speed and skill involved. A polo field (never called a pitch) is the equivalent size of three football pitches, and the ponies (never referred to as horses) go at a serious lick. What is all the more impressive are the players who manage to whack a small white ball with the wide face of a mallet, all at speed on horseback. The game is divided up into seven-minute blasts of play, called 'chukkas', and the aim, as ever, is to score goals. Spectators are famously asked to take to the field and stomp in the divots at half time.

'A GENTLEMAN IS JUST A
GENTLE-MAN – NO MORE, NO LESS;
A DIAMOND POLISHED, THAT WAS
FIRST A DIAMOND IN THE ROUGH.'

**WILLIAM CROSWELL DOANE**

# Acknowledgements

A huge thank you to the incredible Camilla Ackley at Ebury Publishing for hounding and pushing me relentlessly, and to the brilliant Jo Bryant, who has made the whole thing happen. Her encyclopaedic knowledge of gentleman's etiquette, gleaned from her time at Debrett's, is quite extraordinary. I wanted her to make this book fun (I hate boring!) and she has delivered it beautifully. A big thank you to Matt Hollings, the illustrator, for bringing the idiosyncrasies of good dressing visually to life.

I would also like to thank the incredible team at Charles Tyrwhitt. Too numerous to mention them all, but special mention must go to my long-suffering partner in crime Pete Higgins and to Luke Kingsnorth and Joe Irons for their invaluable feedback on the content of this book.

And, of course, to Chrissie Rucker, founder of the White Company and also my wife for keeping me on my toes and for helping me on many occasions to dress the part, and to my children, Tom, Ella, India and Bea who have never held back when it comes to telling me when I cross the line between gentleman and mere mortal.

And to my father, John Wheeler, for making me who I am. He is the consummate gentleman and I have learnt so much from him.